Infant/Toddler Caregiving

A Guide to Creating Partnerships with Families

Developed by
WestEd

for the
California Department of Education

Publishing Information

Infant/Toddler Caregiving: A Guide to Creating Partnerships with Families was developed by WestEd, Sausalito. (See the Acknowledgments on page vii for the names of those who made significant contributions to this guide.) The publication was edited by Faye Ong, working in cooperation with Peter L. Mangione, Janet L. Poole, and Mary Smithberger. It was prepared for photo-offset production by the staff of CDE Press, California Department of Education, with the cover designed by Juan Sanchez.

The guide was published by the California Department of Education, 1430 N Street, Sacramento, CA 95814-5901. It was distributed under the provisions of the Library Distribution Act and *Government Code* Section 11096.

© 1990, 1996, 2005 by the California Department of Education

ISBN 0-8011-0878-0
All rights reserved

Ordering Information

Copies of this publication are available for $18 each, plus shipping and handling charges. California residents are charged sales tax. Orders may be sent to the California Department of Education, CDE Press, Sales Office, 1430 N Street, Suite 3207, Sacramento, CA 95814-5901; FAX (916) 323-0823. See page 92 for complete information on payment, including credit card purchases, and an order blank. Prices on all publications are subject to change.

A list of other infant/toddler caregiving materials available from the Department appears on page 89. In addition, an illustrated *Educational Resources Catalog* describing publications, videos, and other instructional media available from the Department can be obtained without charge by writing to the address given above or by calling the Sales Office at (916) 445-1260.

Photo Credits

The California Department of Education gratefully acknowledges Sheila Signer for the use of all photos but two that appear in this publication; Bonnie Aldridge for the photo on page 25; and Carol Wheeler for the photo on page 81.

Notice

The guidance in *Infant/Toddler Caregiving: A Guide to Creating Partnerships with Families* is not binding on local educational agencies or other entities. Except for the statutes, regulations, and court decisions that are referenced herein, the document is exemplary, and compliance with it is not mandatory. (See *Education Code* Section 33308.5.)

Contents

A Message from the State Superintendent of Public Instruction v

Acknowledgments vii

Introduction 1

Establishment of Positive Child, Family, and Provider Relationships: Vision Statement 3

Section One: Establishing Caregiver-Parent Partnerships 4

    The First Contact 4
    The Entry Decision 5
    Points to Consider 9
    Sample Parent-Caregiver Agreement 10
    Suggested Resources 12

Section Two: Helping Parents Deal with Separation in Child Care 14

    Easing the Separation Process 14
    Understanding the Pain of Separation 17
    Points to Consider 20
    Suggested Resources 20

Section Three: Letting Families Know About You and Your Program 23

    Communication About Your Program 23
    Points to Consider 27
    Suggested Resources 28

Section Four: Listening and Responding to Families 30

    Listening to Parents 30
    Self-awareness in Relating with Others 32
    Points to Consider 40
    Suggested Resources 40

Section Five: Considering the Family in Its Culture 43

    Establishing Communication 43
    Supporting Cultural Diversity 44
    Discomfort About Differences 48
    Shared Experiences and Goals 50
    The Challenge of Diversity 50
    Points to Consider 51
    Suggested Resources 51

Section Six: Involving Parents in the Program 54

    Setting the Stage for Parent Involvement 54
    Parent Involvement in Center and Home Programs 55
    Parent Involvement in Center Programs 57
    Teenage Parent Involvement 60
    Questions Parents May Have About Their
       Involvement in Child Care 61
    Activities for Parents and Children 62
    Other Contributions Parents Can Make to the Program 62
    Points to Consider 62
    Suggested Resources 63

Section Seven: Conducting Business with Families 65

    Financial and Legal Matters 65
    Common Business Problems 66
    Points to Consider 68
    Suggested Resources 68

Section Eight: Helping Families Under Stress 70

    Common Causes of Family Stress 70
    Agencies Helping Families 75
    Points to Consider 76
    Suggested Resources 76

Section Nine: Handling Difficult Issues 79

    Communicating About Difficult Issues 79
    Dealing with Mistreatment of Children 83
    Points to Consider 85
    Suggested Resources 85

A Message from the State Superintendent of Public Instruction

More infants and toddlers than ever before are spending significant amounts of time in child care programs. Yet despite growing public awareness about the critical importance of the first three years of a child's life, many parents still have great difficulty finding safe, healthy, and intellectually engaging programs with well-trained caregivers for their infants and toddlers. As a result, the California Department of Education has embarked on a partnership with WestEd to create the Program for Infant/Toddler Caregivers (PITC), a comprehensive training system with videos, caregiver guides, and trainer's manuals.

Infant/Toddler Caregiving: A Guide to Creating Partnerships with Families is one part of these resources designed to improve the quality of infant/toddler care. This guide presents information that will help caregivers establish and nurture collaborative relationships with the families of infants and toddlers in their programs. Special attention is given to issues that may cause tension for caregivers and family members, issues such as attachment and separation, family stress, and cultural differences.

We encourage child care programs to use this document to guide caregivers in their efforts to create caring partnerships with families and to support family involvement in the program. Thank you for your commitment to the well-being of the infants and toddlers in your care.

JACK O'CONNELL
State Superintendent of Public Instruction

Acknowledgments

This publication was written by Mary B. Lane and Sheila Signer under the direction of J. Ronald Lally. Mary B. Lane directed the first Head Start training program in the San Francisco Bay Area and was the guiding light for the Nurseries in Cross-Cultural Education project funded by the National Institute of Mental Health. Dr. Lane is coauthor of *Human Relations in Teaching* and *Understanding Human Development* and author of numerous articles on working with diverse families in early childhood programs. Among many awards and accolades, Dr. Lane has been honored with a scholarship fund in her name by the East Bay Association for Young Children.

Sheila Signer is a senior program associate with WestEd's Center for Child and Family Studies and a core developer of the Program for Infant/Toddler Caregivers. She studied with Dr. Lane while earning an M.A. at San Francisco State University and worked for many years in the field of family/program relationships.

This publication was developed by the Center for Child and Family Studies, WestEd, under the direction of J. Ronald Lally. Special thanks go to Peter L. Mangione, Carol Young-Holt, Eva Marie Gorman, and Kathleen Bertolucci for editorial assistance; and Virginia Benson, Patricia Gardner, Emily Louw, Janet Poole, Mary Smithberger, and Kathryn Swabel, Child Development Division, California Department of Education, for their review and recommendations on content. Thanks are also extended to the members of the national and California review panels for their comments and suggestions. The national panel members were T. Berry Brazelton, Laura Dittmann, Richard Fiene, Magda Gerber, Asa Hilliard, Alice Honig, Jeree Pawl, Sally Provence, Eleanor Szanton, Yolanda Torres, Bernice Weissbourd, and Donna Wittmer. The California panel members were Dorlene Clayton, Dee Cuney, Ronda Garcia, Jacquelyne Jackson, Lee McKay, Janet Nielsen, Pearlene Reese, Maria Ruiz, June Sale, Patty Siegel, and Lenore Thompson.

Introduction

When a very young child enters child care, both the infant and the infant's family experience dramatic changes in their lives. The infant is faced, usually for the first time, with the challenge of adapting to a strange environment, different routines, and new relationships. The parents, too, must make a difficult adjustment—the sharing of the care of their child with someone outside the family.

Parents enrolling infants in child care for the first time usually appreciate the help and the time made available to them by professional caregivers. At the same time, they are almost sure to be worried. Will the caregiver genuinely care for and about their infant as they would? Parents seek a person to whom they can entrust their infant, knowing that the child will be safe and cared for. They need someone who will understand their messages—someone who will respect their feelings and choices about the infant's care. Finally, the parents need caregivers who will provide the consistency between in-home and out-of-home care that every infant needs in order to thrive.

As infant/toddler caregivers try to fulfill all these expectations, they are faced with a challenge. The caregiver and the infant's family must develop a partnership, a cooperative venture on the child's behalf.

Sensitivity to and awareness of parents' feelings, as well as the caregiver's own feelings, are basic to the process of building a relationship with the infant's family. Thoughtful caregivers know that parents of infants entering child care often experience a variety of emotions; they learn not to take it personally when parents express their anxieties. The parents, as well as the child, need reassurance. Professional caregivers who define their role as one of support to the family, rather than that of a substitute parent, will go a long way in providing this reassurance.

The bonds between the parents and infant or toddler need support from the caregiver, particularly during the first few months of care when the family and child are adjusting to the new situation. Closeness between the infant and his or her family is basic to the child's healthy emotional development and to the par-

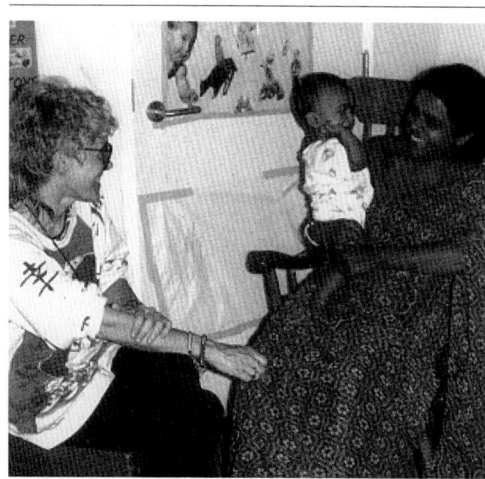

ents' emotional well-being, as well. In addition, the loving relationships an infant forms with parents and other family members provide the foundation for other close relationships in the infant's life, including his or her relationships with professional caregivers.

Expressions of support for the infant's attachment to family members will help to ease parental anxieties about using out-of-home care. Parents who see that the bonds between child care and their child complement, rather than compete with, existing family bonds will also be more likely to discuss with caregivers child-rearing issues that trouble them. They will trust that their child's caregiver respects their parental role.

Both the infant's need for consistent nurturance and the parents' need for reassurance call for continuing communication and cooperation between parents and caregivers. Yet in some cases, the family may not even speak the same language as the caregiver. Some families' life-styles may differ greatly from that of the caregiver. Families may be troubled by problems of child abuse or neglect, physical or mental disabilities, homelessness or poverty.

No matter what the circumstances or cultural background of the families served, the development of a partnership with parents is an essential ingredient of quality care for the child. The more resourceful the caregiver is in encouraging the family's participation in the child's care, the more positive the child care experience will be for the infant or toddler.

The possibilities for family involvement in an infant/toddler care program are almost limitless. Parties and celebrations, parent participation in or observation of children's groups, classes and workshops for family members and staff on the child care site, discussion groups on topics of special concern, fund-raising activities, building or repairing toys—all these contribute to feelings of connection between the families served and the program staff.

Even more important are informal types of involvement that the child's parents (or other family caregivers) experience on a daily basis. Friendly conversations and discussions during drop-off and pickup times help parents feel welcome and valued in the program. A caregiver's offer of a cup of coffee at the end of the day can be the encouragement a parent needs to bring up a troubling problem with his or her child's behavior. The caregiver may find in the occasion an opportunity to broach a sensitive topic to the parent. Cordial, informal interactions reinforce the parent-caregiver partnership and contribute to the development of a relationship of trust.

Caregivers who welcome parents into their programs will usually find them open to involvement in their child's care. Establishing a supportive give-and-take relationship with parents, however, takes skill, planning, and preparation. This guide will assist caregivers in creating partnerships with families—relationships built on mutual trust and respect which will not only support the child and the parents but also the caregiver.

Establishment of Positive Child, Family, and Provider Relationships

Vision Statement

The caregiver maintains an open, friendly, and cooperative relationship with each child's family, encourages the family's involvement in the program, and supports the child's relationship with the family.

Today's families take many different forms. Single mothers or fathers, both parents, or stepparents may share responsibility for their children with grandparents, uncles, aunts, sisters, or brothers. The caregiver and parents become partners who communicate openly and respectfully about a variety of concerns. Thus, the caregiver is able to discuss problem behavior with parents in a constructive, supportive manner; respect each family's cultural background, religious beliefs, and child-rearing practices; and develop strong, caring relationships with children while at the same time supporting family bonds. Caregivers also recognize that parenthood, too, is a developmental process and that they can support parents in that role.

Young infants are establishing patterns of sleeping, waking, eating, playing, and relating to others. They can be supported in developing some stability in those routines by the sensitive and consistent responses of adults. Parents and caregivers can respond more appropriately to the infant's signals when they share details with each other about the child's day: sleeping, eating, and diapering routines; activities; and moods.

Mobile infants may have difficulty separating from the parents, even when the caregiver is a familiar and trusted person. Caregivers and parents need to discuss ways of handling this problem and recognize that separation may be upsetting for both parent and child. Caregivers should recognize the potential for competition between themselves and parents and work to avoid it. Caregivers and parents also need to agree on reasonable and safe limits as children begin to explore and wander.

Toddlers develop their own special routines to feel more organized and secure. Parents and caregivers need to share a common understanding of the child's patterns and provide constant, dependable support for the toddler's growth toward self-definition.

This statement is an excerpt from Vision VIII in *Visions for Infant/Toddler Care: Guidelines for Professional Caregiving* (Sacramento: California Department of Education, 1988). The *Visions* document outlines the visions or goals of The Program for Infant/Toddler Caregivers.

Section One:
Establishing Caregiver-Parent Partnerships

A partnership between caregivers and parents makes good sense. After all, each partner has an important yet distinctly different role in the child's life. Furthermore, infants and toddlers need the consistency and predictability that can come only from caregivers and families working together.

This type of partnership does not just happen. Both parties must have the desire to provide the best possible care for the infant or toddler. Parents and caregivers need to share information continually and to discuss and review their agreed-on goals for the infant in terms of his or her daily experiences. An atmosphere of open communication must be created—and it begins with the first contact.

The First Contact

The quality of the first contact will set the tone for your ongoing relationship if the parent decides to enroll the child in your program. Your relationship may begin with a phone call from the prospective parent to your child care program. The parent will want to know whether there are vacancies and will probably ask a few questions about the ages and number of children served, costs, and hours of service.

Request a face-to-face interview with the family members responsible for the child's care. Explain that you are interested in hearing what the family expects of child care and wish to learn about the child through the family's eyes. Let the parent know that you would like to discuss your philosophy of child care and the way your program operates. For the first meeting, you will need a quiet place to sit where you can talk with few interruptions. At this time, you will be explor-

A child enrolled is a family enrolled.

ing whether the program matches the family's needs closely enough to pursue the relationship. You will also have your first opportunity to introduce the concept of a partnership.

Describe to parents how your roles will complement each other:

- The family is enlisting a professional partner to help nurture and educate their child as well as to meet a pragmatic family need.
- Enrollment in child care may be seen as an early step toward broadening the child's social and educational experiences.
- Using child care is not a "giving up," but rather an expanding process, expanding the family's scope of influence as well as the child's environment.

The first visit is a good time to present written material about program operations. Written information should include: (1) philosophy; (2) procedures;

(3) policies; and (4) expectations for family participation.

Remember that words can be tricky. No matter how carefully worded written statements are, they can be misunderstood. During the entry interview be sure that you cover all important topics verbally, and clarify written information before misunderstandings occur. Avoid painting a perfect picture of the care that is given, but emphasize the commitment to quality.

The Grand Tour

Nothing will communicate a program's dedication to the well-being of children more than a walk through the program environment. Here is an opportunity to point out your health and safety practices. Drawing attention to the health and safety features will help to relieve some of the concerns parents have about leaving their children in care.

Point out how the environment is arranged for safe and hygienic practices. Show the caregiver who is changing a diaper and using the proper sanitation procedures. Parents will be reassured to learn that caregivers are trained to set up and maintain a clean, safe, and healthy environment, as well as to administer first aid and cardiopulmonary resuscitation (CPR).

Make outdoor space part of the tour. Point out how it is arranged for both safety and free exploration. Because fresh air and natural light contribute to the healthy growth and development of infants and toddlers, emphasize the importance of contact with nature. Describe how outdoor playtime is arranged and supervised. If you have limited or no outdoor space, explain how you use any existing space and how you arrange for the children to experience other outdoor areas.

The Entry Decision

After the parents have had a chance to read your materials about the program, made a few visits to the program, and clarified any of their questions about program operations, they will decide whether your program is right for them and their child. If they decide to enroll the child, the next step is the entry process. Explain to them that this process is a gradual one which will require their participation if the child is to make a good adjustment to the program. Describe to them your program's philosophy of entry into care and the specific role you expect them to play.

Addressing Special Concerns

Each family will have specific concerns which need to be addressed. The child may need to have or to avoid certain foods. Special arrangements for pickup, transportation, or other issues may be required. Future misunderstandings can be avoided if you and the family work out these arrangements before the beginning weeks of care. Arrangements need to be spelled out in a written agreement that is

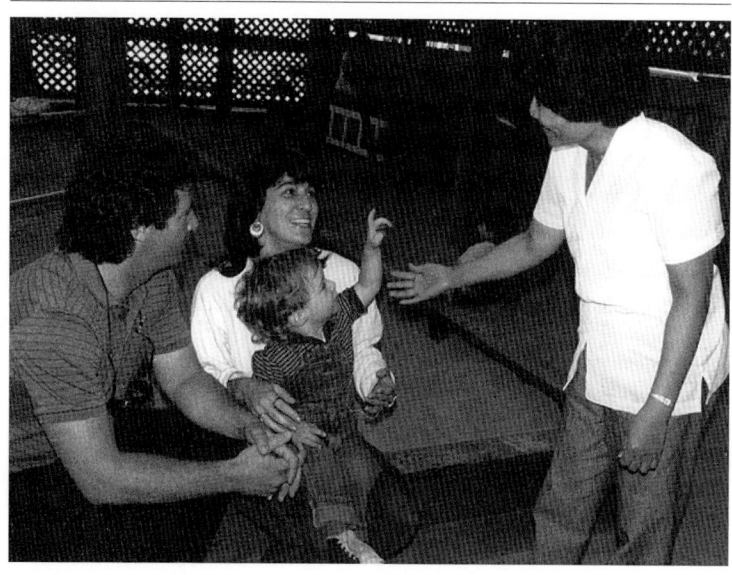

clear and seems fair to both partners. Of course, this agreement can be altered as needs change, but clear agreements from the start can head off many potential sources of tension between families and child care staff.

Business Arrangements

Some matters must be discussed in advance or else problems will almost always arise. These matters include:

- Fee arrangements
- Time responsibilities
- Daily information exchange
- Health policies and emergency planning

Fee Arrangements

In a center program, the program manager usually handles the fees; in a family child care home, it is the caregiver's responsibility to communicate in writing what the program expects. Communication about fees should be friendly but very explicit. If continually late payments may be cause for terminating the child's enrollment, this possibility should be stated clearly at the time of enrollment. A sample parent-caregiver agreement is provided at the end of this section.

Time Responsibilities

Deciding what time the child is dropped off and picked up at child care, how long the parent stays with the child at those times, and how much additional time parents will spend in involvement in the program are important issues on which you and the parents must agree.

Arrival and Departure Times. One area that can cause friction between caregivers and parents is the timing of dropping off and picking up the child. Not many situations frustrate a parent on the way to work more than waiting for a tardy early-shift caregiver to come and unlock a center or a family home provider who is not at home when expected. Similarly, caregivers often feel irritated or frustrated when a parent arrives 20 or 30 minutes after closing time.

Partnerships require flexibility.

Inconsistent drop-off and pickup times can also be an issue. For example, some caregivers prefer that children arrive at about the same time each day they are in care. Parents, particularly parents of young infants, may need more flexible schedules. A solution is needed that will be comfortable for both the caregiver and the parent. The issue of irregular schedules can be seen in a positive way—as an opportunity for you and the parent to refine your partnership.

The first step is to find out why the parent prefers to keep an irregular schedule with the infant. The mother of a young infant, for example, may really wish she could stay at home with her infant. She may want to take advantage of every chance to be with him or her. Varying work hours or other scheduling issues may make it inconvenient for a toddler's parent to bring the child at a regular time. Parents with jobs are often juggling a variety of time constraints. Take the time to really understand how the parent feels.

After you have listened to the parent's point of view, it is your turn to express your own preference. If you find it difficult to accommodate the parent's irregular schedule, give reasons for your preference. You may feel that babies usually do better when they follow regular routines. You may feel better able to attend to the needs of each child and parent when arrival times are prearranged. In any case, be sure that you are clear with the parent about where you stand on the issue and why.

Finally, you will need to negotiate a solution. Perhaps the infant's mother would be willing to arrive at a regular time but remain with her infant in the group. Another possibility is to make a formal agreement about when the child will come on designated days so that you will know what time to expect him or her each day.

Even when a parent does not want to commit to a regular schedule at first, the issue may work itself out over time. Once the child is well integrated into the program, the parent may prefer a more regular schedule. The important thing is that you will have communicated your desire to support the parent's relationship with the child.

Allowing Time for the Transition. Parents and caregivers also need to reach an understanding about how much time the parent should spend when dropping off and picking up the child. The caregiver and the parent should plan ahead for a smooth, relaxed transition. As in setting arrival and departure times, coming to an agreement on this issue requires careful listening, clear communication, and tactful negotiation.

Parent Involvement. Some caregiving settings, particularly parent cooperatives and Head Start programs, expect more time from parents. If parents are expected to observe, help out in some way, or even share in the care, they need to know specifically just how much time is required or desired. If parent group participation, fundraising, or other forms of program advocacy are expected, discuss these expectations with parents. Through your discussions, seek as close an alignment as possible between the needs of your program and what the parent is willing to do.

Daily Information Exchange

Infants and toddlers develop so rapidly that there is something new to report almost every day. Let parents know that they will need to allow time for a daily exchange of information. Parents need to relay pertinent information to caregivers when they drop off their child, such as a bad night the infant had, medicine to be given, or any family emergency or event which affects the infant. Similarly, at the end of the day, the caregiver needs time to fill the parent in about the child's day.

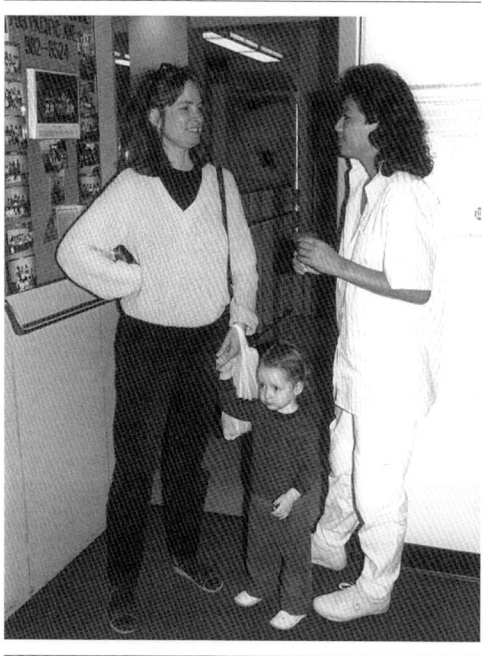

In addition, caregivers and parents need to keep each other posted on the infant's latest developments in order to coordinate their efforts to support the child's growth—and also to share the joys of that growth.

Infants are now known to be much more aware of what goes on around them than previously thought. Let parents know how much the child learns from

Parents enjoy hearing about their children.

exploring objects and areas. Sharing information about a child's development might include reporting a toddler's progress toward toilet learning, but also includes reporting on an infant's mood or social development. For example, when Yolanda comes to pick up her six-week-old baby, Cecilia's caregiver tells her, "You know what? Cecilia smiled at me today!"

The daily exchange also provides you with the opportunity to share what you know about infant development as it applies to each parent's child. For example, with a parent whose child is beginning to exhibit "stranger anxiety," you can discuss how infants often develop a fear of strangers when they are six to nine months old. You can help the parent of a toddler to understand how important it is for that child to express a budding sense of independence by saying no.

Although both drop-off and pickup times are important opportunities for parents and caregivers to share information about the child, work with parents to agree on one of these times for more extensive discussions. Evenings are usually better for parents because they are not hurrying on the way to work. This is the time to discuss special topics and pass out information about meetings, forms to be filled out, and the like. However, at the end of the day, the child may be tired, impatient to go home, or unwilling to wait one more moment for parental attention.

Try to arrange opportunities for open-ended communication. If the child is able to wait comfortably, perhaps absorbed in his or her own play, you may be able to talk with the parent while you pick up toys together. You may have a chance to sit and converse over a cup of coffee. These times help to reinforce the child's awareness of your partnership with the child's parent, thus strengthening the child's feelings of trust in the child care setting.

Health Policies and Emergency Planning

One of the most important ways caregivers can assist parents is by being supportive when infants are ill. You can help the parents feel less anxious by being clear about the program's health policies and by sharing with them how other parents and children have coped with similar illnesses.

Caregivers become skilled, through years of experience, at recognizing the early symptoms of illness. They can alert parents to indications that the infant may be getting sick, such as unusual fussiness, lethargic behavior, or refusal to take a bottle.

Because caregivers and parents have to rely on each other so that the overall care of the infant is handled well, both partners have to plan for emergencies. What happens when a caregiver gets sick? A child gets hurt or becomes ill during the day? A parent's car breaks down?

Backup plans need to be developed for these situations and other emergencies. The parent should have a plan that includes a minimum of two, preferably three, individuals who can step in at a moment's notice and assume the parental role.

Through the entry interview, written materials, and daily reports to the parents, caregivers have the opportunity to establish a partnership with parents from the very beginning of their relationship. They can share their own philosophy of care, feelings, and concerns and also learn about the philosophy and attitudes which underlie the parents' child-rearing practices and expectations. Expressing and being open to ideas and feelings can make it easier for caregivers to maintain a program where everyone feels comfortable.

Points to Consider

1. What are some steps you can take when a parent asks you for information about your program to set a positive tone of partnership from the beginning of your relationship? In what ways can you communicate the program's policies and philosophy so that the parent can make an informed decision?

2. How could you be better prepared to communicate information about your program to parents? Do you have up-to-date written materials to give to them? Does your parent's handbook or brochure set the tone you wish to convey about your program?

3. Do you make the effort to engage parents in conversations about their child every day? What are the important things to communicate? What are some of the things you can learn about the child which will help your day with the child to go more smoothly? Are you sensitive to the parents' schedules, keeping longer conversations for times when they are not in a hurry?

4. What are some of the ways you can help parents understand that they are the most important adults in their child's life? Do you recognize signs of concern in parents about this issue? What are some ways in which you can support the family bond?

5. Do you involve parents in decisions about the program's care for their child? To what extent can you accommodate parents' wishes, even when they may not coincide with your regular way of doing things?

Sample Parent-Caregiver Agreement

Parent's name: _____ Child's name: _____

Name of business: _____ Telephone: _____

Address of workplace: _____

Welcome to my (our) family child care home (child care center).

The state of _____ does (not) require a license for this business. I (we) do (not) participate in the USDA Child Care Food Program.

The purpose of this contract is to define the mutual terms of agreement for child care arrangements.
It is your responsibility to let me (us) know of any changes of address or telephone and emergency numbers.
Parents are welcome to visit at any time.

Hours and Days of Operation

Child care services will begin on _____ 20____.

The hours for care will begin at _____ and end at _____ on the following days: _____

If the child is going to be absent or late, please call in advance.

Child care will not be available on the following holidays: _____

Family Child Care Home Only

My vacation period will be _____. You will be responsible for making other child care arrangements.

I may find it necessary to use the services of a substitute caregiver on occasion. My substitute is: _____
_____.

Rates

$_____ per week for full-time care (7 or more hours).

$_____ per hour for regular part-time care (less than 4 hours).

$_____ per hour for drop-in care if space is available.

$_____ for late fee. This fee will be charged for any time after _____ unless special arrangements have been made.

$_____ per meal. Parents are required to bring the appropriate foods for infants under _____ months old.

Child care fees are payable in advance and are due no later than _____. An additional fee of $_____ will be charged if the payment is late. Fees may be paid:

        Weekly _____   Bi-weekly _____   Monthly _____

An advance deposit of $_____ must be paid at the time of enrollment. This amount will be returned when services are terminated.

Fees may be (or may not be) adjusted when services are not available because of illness or vacation by either party.

Child care fees will be paid by: cash_____

                             check_____

> NOTICE: A two-week written notice is required for any of the following:
> 1. Termination of the agreement by either party
> 2. Increases in child care fees
> 3. Vacation periods for both parents and caregiver

Food

Meals will be: _____ prepared by the program _____ brought by parent.

Meals served will be: _____ breakfast _____ lunch _____ snack _____ supper _____ evening snack. Please explain if the child has special dietary needs.

Infants will be fed according to the parent's instructions. Parents must update and notify caregiver of any changes in feeding schedules, formulas, and additional foods. Milk will be furnished for all infants who no longer need a special formula. Breast-fed infants should have an adequate supply of expressed milk in bottles.

Medical Information

Your child is required to have a physical examination:_____ before admission in this child care program.

                                                   _____ each year while enrolled.

Please notify me (us) if your child will be absent because of illness. If your child is home for more than _____ days, he or she must bring a signed physician's report when returning to the program.

Contagious diseases must be brought to my (our) attention immediately. All families involved will be notified. Medication will be administered only if there is a signed permission form from a licensed physician.

If your child becomes ill during care, you will be asked to pick up your child immediately. If you cannot be reached, I (we) will call one of the emergency numbers you have listed. Your child will be readmitted when symptoms have subsided.

Clothing

Your child's clothing and other items must be labeled with his or her name and brought in some type of storage bag. Parents will supply at least two complete sets of play clothes, outdoor clothing, and the following:

_____ disposable diapers   _____ baby wipes   _____ bibs

_____ cloth diapers   _____ training pants   _____ plastic pants

Field Trips

We may sometimes take trips away from the child care setting to provide children with special experiences. I (We) will need your permission to allow your child to ride in a car or public transportation. You will be notified in advance when trips are being planned.

Our state _____ does _____ does not require a proper infant seat for car travel. _____ You _____ I (We) will provide the equipment.

I (we) fully understand and agree to the terms of this contract. This agreement may be renegotiated at any time.

Parent's signature _____ Date _____

Caregiver's signature _____ Date _____

Suggested Resources

Books and Articles

Boyce, Carol Gratsch. "Trading Control for Partnership: Guidelines for Developing Parent Ownership in Your Program," *Child Care Information Exchange,* Vol. 144 (March/April 2002), 75–78.

Explains the importance of promoting parent ownership in a cooperative early childhood program. Touches on decision making, classroom involvement, friendly interactions, goal setting, and staff attitudes.

Brazelton, T. Berry. *Working and Caring.* Boston, Mass.: Addison-Wesley Longman, 2000.

Provides helpful information for working parents and caregivers on the stresses working parents experience.

Brazelton, T. Berry, and Stanley I. Greenspan. *The Irreducible Needs of Children: What Every Child Must Have to Grow, Learn, and Flourish.* Boulder, Colo.: Perseus Book Group, 2000.

Explores seven needs of infants and young children that, when met by families and professional caregivers, provide the fundamental building blocks for children's higher-level emotional, social, and intellectual abilities.

Carter, Margie. "Communicating with Parents," *Child Care Information Exchange,* Vol. 110 (July/August 1996), 80–83.

Offers five strategies for enhancing communication, including keeping parents well informed; helping parents to introduce themselves in the classroom; and creating dialogue in newsletters and bulletins.

Copeland, Margaret Leitch, and Barbara S. McCreedy. "Creating Family-Friendly Policies: Are Child Care Center Policies in Line with Current Family Realities?" *Child Care Information Exchange,* Vol. 113 (January/February 1997), 7–10.

Addresses current issues, such as corporate downsizing, flex time, and blended families, and the effects on emerging child care needs. Suggests that child care programs update policies by examining staff attitudes, evaluating enrollment policies, and offering more flexibility and support to parents.

Cunningham, Bruce. "The Good Business of Being Father-Friendly: Does Your Center Welcome Male Customers?" *Child Care Information Exchange,* Vol. 135 (September/October 2000), 70–71.

Offers suggestions for making child care programs welcoming to fathers and other men involved in the care of young children. Describes six areas of father-friendly service.

Dodge, Diane Trister. "Sharing Your Program with Families," *Child Care Information Exchange*, Vol. 101 (1995), 7–11.

Offers guidelines for child care providers in working with parents to achieve mutual goals. Focuses on goals for the curriculum and ongoing communication with families.

From Neurons to Neighborhoods: The Science of Early Childhood Development. Edited by Deborah A. Phillips and Jack Shonkoff. Washington, D.C.: National Academy Press, 2000.

Reports on an extensive review of scientific research and child policy centered on child development from birth to age five. Contains ten core concepts, including one that states "Human development is shaped by a dynamic and continuous interaction between biology and experience."

Gonzalez-Mena, Janet, and Dianne W. Eyer. *Infants, Toddlers, and Caregivers*. Mountain View, Calif.: Mayfield Publishing Co., 2000.

This expanded edition includes sections on parent-caregiver relationships, the nine-month separation in child care, and multicultural situations.

Greenman, James. "Beyond Family Friendly: The Family Center," *Child Care Information Exchange,* Vol. 114 (March/April 1997), 66–69.

Advocates the creation of family-care centers that focus on the family's economic and psychological security and the relationships that promote well-being as well as on the child's security, health, and development.

Miller, Karen. "Caring for the Little Ones—Developing a Collaborative Relationship with Parents," *Child Care Information Exchange*, Vol. 135 (September/October 2000), 86–88.

Discusses the benefits of collaborative relationships with parents and provides suggestions for developing rapport and offering support.

Audiovisuals

Protective Urges: Working with the Feelings of Parents and Caregivers. Sacramento: California Department of Education, 1996. Video, 27 minutes.

Available in English, Spanish, and Chinese (Cantonese) versions, this video deals with the strong emotions parents and caregivers feel about protecting and nurturing very young children. Caregivers learn how to help ease parents' concerns about using infant care by communicating understanding, competence, and honesty. They also learn about a four-step process for exploring, accepting, and dealing with their own feelings. A video magazine is included.

Section Two:
Helping Parents Deal with Separation in Child Care

More tears have been shed over separation than over any other area of child care. These tears are not limited to those of infants and toddlers; they include those of mothers, fathers, and sometimes grandmas and Aunt Susies. For caregivers, too, separation issues are among the most stressful to deal with. Some infants and toddlers seem to adjust to a new setting with relative ease, while others continue to be upset by separation for weeks or even months.

Parents also vary in the degree of discomfort they feel about leaving an infant or toddler in child care. This discomfort is often related to the degree of difficulty the child experiences. The anxiety of the parent will be felt by the child who will, in turn, feel more anxious—and vice versa.

Easing the Separation Process

Caregivers can help in the separation process by involving parents. Those parents who take steps to assist in their child's adjustment will be better able to cope with their own feelings. When parents see that they have the power to help their child, they will not feel so helpless and guilty. You can assist parents and children with separation in the following ways:

- Assign a primary caregiver.
- Encourage parents to prepare their child before arrival at the child care setting.

- Allow time for the transition between the home and the child care program.
- Help the parent and child with the initial separation.

Assign a Primary Caregiver

A very important early step in the entry process is the development of a personal bond between the family and the program. If there is more than one caregiver in the program, make clear who is primarily responsible for the child's care to the parent, the caregivers, and, in time, to the child.

The primary caregiver will be a great support to both parent and child. The infant or toddler will develop bonds of familiarity and trust sooner if there is one special caregiver with major responsibility for attending to his or her needs during the day. Parents will also feel more secure knowing they can talk to the same person each day.

The primary caregiver will be reporting to parents any major changes in the child's appetite, bowel movements, napping, and general state of being, such as fussiness or lethargic behavior. This caregiver will also be the person who will soon know the infant well enough to notice the important milestones in the child's development that parents love to hear about, such as pulling up, rolling over, a new tooth, a new word, or a first step. The primary caregiver's knowledge of the special characteristics of each child will reassure parents that their child is in good hands.

Encourage Parents to Prepare Their Child

Encourage parents to talk with their child about child care before entering the program. Of course, how parents talk about child care and how far in advance they do it will depend on the age of the child. To a young infant, they might say on the first morning of child care, "I'm taking you to Bonnie's house. She is going to take care of you for a while. I think you are going to like Bonnie."

A toddler may be interested in hearing that "there are going to be other children there for you to play with," and can be told a day or two ahead of time as well as on the first day of care. The parent's words are less important than the tone of voice, which reassures the child that "everything is going to be okay. You are going to be safe and happy in child care. This change will be good for us."

Allow Time for the Transition Between Home and the Child Care Program

The next step is to help parents see that time spent with the child in the caregiving setting at the beginning will pay off in a smoother adjustment in the long run. During repeated visits, the infant will have a chance to get used to the environment. Explain to parents that it is common for children to be upset during this transition period. Reassure them that children usually make a good adjustment.

Parents will feel more relaxed about the entry process if you provide them with a timetable for the transition. This timetable actually begins with the initial visits of the child and parent during the process of selecting a child care program. Early visits should be occasions for friendly exchanges between you and the parent. The child needs to see that the parent is comfortable with you and that you and the parent are enjoying each other. Hearing laughter and friendly conversation between the parent and the caregiver is reassuring to a child in a new setting, especially when he or she is not being pressured to leave the parent or to relate to the caregiver or the other children.

After the child has had one or two visits in the new setting with the parent

present, the timetable continues with the parent leaving the child in care for an hour or so. During the first week or two, the child should be left in care for increasing periods of time. The parent should stay longer than the usual five or ten minutes when dropping off or picking up the child and arrive early to pick up the child at the end of the day. Watching other parents and children coming and going can be difficult for an infant or toddler who is just learning about separation, so caregivers need to explain this to the parent.

Not all parents are able to meet these standards for easing a child into care. Many, however, will inquire about child care before they return to jobs outside the home. Encourage these parents to begin the adjustment process with their child at least two weeks before they need full-time care.

Parents who are already employed and who need immediate child care are often able to arrange for extra time with their child if they understand its importance. Some parents, however, will find it impossible to comply with the recommended timetable. They may need your help in negotiating a reasonable compromise between the demands of their job and the needs of their child. Even when parents cannot take time off from work, encourage them to prepare the child by talking about child care during commuting times. You can also help parents by reassuring them that their child will be okay.

Help the Parent and Child with the Initial Separation

The first moments of separation can be an upsetting time for parents as well as infants. The primary caregiver can ease the separation for both by allowing the infant or toddler time to warm up to the new setting. How this can be done is the subject of the video, *First Moves: Welcoming a Child to a New Caregiving Setting*. (See Suggested Resources at the end of this section.)

Remember that babies are adept at picking up the emotional tone of a situation. Therefore, if a parent or caregiver feels hurried or harassed when dropping off or picking up the child, the infant will sense this. The tension will actually make separation more difficult for the infant once the shift in care occurs. On the other hand, a parent or caregiver should not drag out the last moments of the transition. Once the parent has begun to leave, good-byes should be said and the parent should leave promptly.

Some parents, especially when they are new to a program, feel so ambivalent about leaving the child that they start to leave and then come back. Others want to avoid upsetting the child when they go and prefer to leave with no good-bye. Explain to parents that these behaviors are confusing to children and prolong the anxiety of separation, while a cheerful farewell and speedy exit will help the child to accept the situation. To assist in the moment of separation, insist that parents say good-bye to their child. You can reassure parents by explaining that the infant often stops crying soon after Mom or Dad is out of sight.

Understanding the Pain of Separation

No matter how carefully parents, caregivers, and program directors plan for the initial event, there is bound to be some discomfort in the process of separation. Much of this is related to the mixed

---

Good-byes build trust.

---

feelings that many parents have when they place their child, especially an infant or young toddler, in daily care with someone new. And the pangs of separation do not just occur in the beginning; difficulties can arise for either parent or child long after the entry period is over.

Caregivers can be most helpful to the parent and child when they understand the feelings that make separation difficult for parents. Here is an example of a mother who is anxious about using child care for her baby:

The Initial Separation

Rosa carefully fastens the strap to Tony's car seat. With a guilty look toward the back seat, she heads toward the home of the provider she has chosen to take care of her baby, a mile from her own home. She drives slowly, almost as if she doesn't really want to go there. She is close to tears.

Am I doing the right thing? she asks herself. *Maybe I should have stayed home with Tony, but I need to work. Will he cry when I leave? Will he remember me when I come back? I sure hate to miss seeing when he first starts to crawl, when he takes his first step. . . . How can I do this? What do I really know about Maria's infant care program, anyway? Well, here we are, Tony boy. Let's try it for a week, anyway.*

These are the thoughts that preoccupy Rosa on her way to Maria's family child care home. In order to win Rosa's trust, as well as that of three-month-old Tony, the caregiver will need to show an awareness of Rosa's difficulty in leaving him. Rosa's feelings may have little to do with the caregiver or the quality of care she provides, but more to do with Rosa's own feelings of anxiety and guilt. Rosa has chosen infant care for Tony because she sees no other option. She is in no way certain that it will be good for him.

Maria can help to put Rosa at ease during this stage of separation. "I guess this is a big day for you and Tony, isn't it?" she says when they arrive. Maria's tone tells Rosa that she realizes Rosa feels torn. Her voice expresses empathy without talking directly about the sensitive issue.

Maria continues with, "It's great that you can stay for a couple of hours this morning. Tony will feel better if he can take this change in his life in little steps." This statement tells Rosa that she is able to help Tony with his adjustment while reinforcing the importance of Rosa's role as parent. Rosa begins to see that she is among people who care about her and her baby's feelings.

Tony, at three months of age, will probably separate from his mother without much distress. He has not yet developed "stranger anxiety," and by the time he is six months old, Maria's house will seem like another home to him. She will no longer be a stranger. She will be a friend.

Later Separation Issues

Rosa can relax now. She has found a caring person to turn her baby over to each work morning. She is comfortable with Maria's home; Tony is developing well and seems to love child care. The crisis may come for Rosa when Tony is about nine months to a year old and she finds that he does not want to go home with her when she comes to pick him up. He cries when he has to leave.

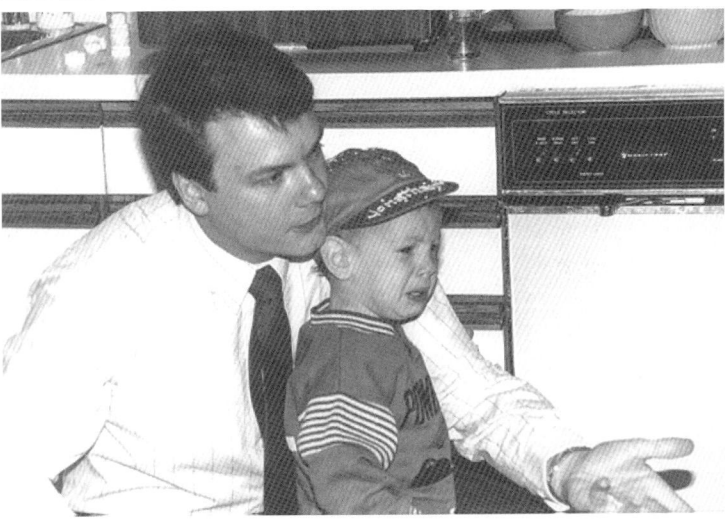

This may awaken the feelings of guilt that had died down while Rosa was congratulating herself on having found good child care for her infant. Now she may wonder if Tony's behavior is telling her that he feels she has neglected him. She may ask herself, *Does he love Maria more than he loves me?*

This is Maria's chance to help Rosa and Tony with another step in their adjustment to her program. She can tell Rosa that this is normal behavior for a child who is learning about separation. Perhaps Rosa can play with Tony in the child care environment for a few minutes before attempting to take him home. He may need time to complete the activity that he was engaged in when his mother arrived.

The caregiver can also suggest that this may be an appropriate time in Tony's life for a visit to Rosa's workplace. She can ask Rosa to bring a photograph of herself to be taped up on Tony's cubby. Most important, she can reaffirm to Rosa the importance of both home and child care in Tony's life and remind her that his well-being represents a caring partnership between them.

Conflicting Feelings

Of course, no two parents have exactly the same feelings about using child care. Parents feel uncomfortable about using child care for many reasons. Listen carefully and use your observation skills to learn about the parents' specific circumstances, feelings, and needs.

In contrast to Rosa who has to work to survive economically, Jackie is a professional woman who wants a family but does not wish to interrupt her career. When baby Beverly was six weeks old, Jackie was ready to go back to work.

Jackie has conflicting goals. She wants Beverly to have the best in life, but she finds that staying at home to care for her is tedious. She is eager to return to her law office, yet she wonders whether Beverly is losing out on an important part of her life by not having her mother's care every day. Once Jackie is back at work, her conflicting feelings cause her to be distracted at work, irritable at home, and anxious at the infant program where Beverly is enrolled. The time she does spend with Beverly is not as rewarding as it could be because of the tension Jackie feels about her parental role.

The caregiver's role with this mother will be quite different from that with Rosa. Here, she needs to help Jackie understand that it is not necessary for a mother to be available 24 hours a day to her baby in order to develop and maintain the important bond between mother and child. The caregiver may suggest that Jackie spend some time talking with another mother who has experienced similar feelings.

Books, videos, and other resources that the caregiver can recommend or lend to Jackie will also help her to see that her goal of a career need not conflict with having a family. Or the caregiver might refer Jackie to a community resource that specializes in helping mothers like Jackie who are struggling with their feelings.

Other concerns can create conflicts in parents who leave their infants and toddlers in child care. Some parents may fear that they will be criticized if they expose their child-rearing practices to public view. Others, like Rosa, may fear that "my baby" may come to love and enjoy the caregiver "more than he loves me."

If the infant or toddler has a difficult adjustment, parents may worry that the caregiver will dislike their child. Parents may feel uncomfortable about what neighbors, friends, and family think about

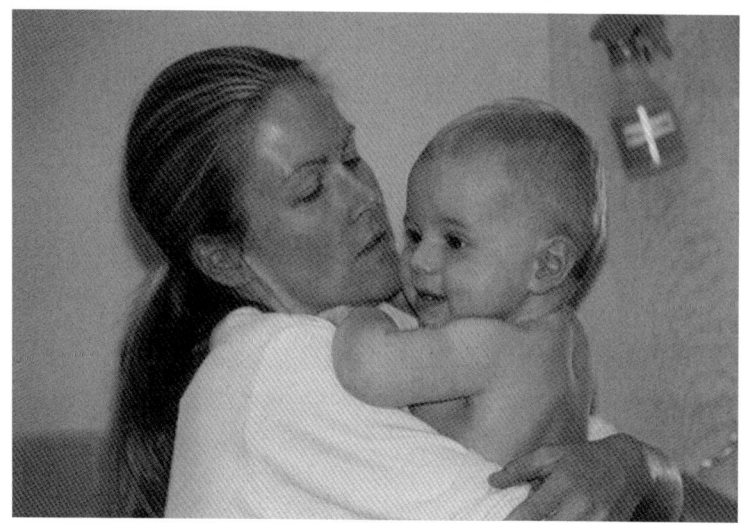

their leaving the baby in the care of others. Or, like Jackie, they may feel confusion about values and ask, "Am I being selfish to put the professional stimulation I get from my job ahead of staying home and caring for my baby?"

Adjustment to child care is an ongoing process.

Many parents will feel anxious about the quality of child care their children will receive, what lessons they will learn, and how they will be treated. Many also feel anxious about the safety of their infants and toddlers. Protecting their young children from accidents, neglect, and abuse is a basic responsibility of parents and one which they have been doing since the moment of that child's birth. Parents will naturally feel some anxiety and guilt when they cannot personally provide this protection.

Help Parents with Conflicting Feelings

Caregivers can help parents feel more comfortable about using infant and toddler care in the following ways:

1. Recognize that parents' discomfort is natural and to be expected, and communicate this to parents who are experiencing difficulties. Parents are often comforted by the knowledge that they are not different from other parents.
2. Be generous in your communication of reassurance and information. Assure parents that caregivers really care and are capable of handling separation without damage to the child.
3. Be honest. Avoid leading parents to believe that separation is easy for children after six months of age.
4. Talk to parents about the behaviors to expect from the infant during the early days of separation, and advise patience.
5. Tell parents about your feelings if you have had similar experiences with your own children.
6. Suggest that a parent seek out another parent who has overcome his or her feelings of guilt and anxiety.
7. Point out cues from the infant's behavior that show the infant is happy, healthy, and growing.
8. Remember that your attitude can make a difference.

Good feelings are contagious. If you feel comfortable and certain that the program is a good place for children and families, parents will catch the positive feeling and pass it on to their children.

Points to Consider

1. From the beginning of the entry process, how can you help parents understand the parent-child separation process? What are some things parents can do to help their child accept separation?
2. If your program has more than one caregiver, is a caregiver chosen at the time of entry who will have primary responsibility for the newly enrolled child? Is that caregiver given primary responsibility for communicating with the child's parents?
3. What are some ways you can help parents and their child at the moment of saying good-bye?
4. Do you encourage parents to spend some time with the child in the child care setting when they are dropping off or picking up their child? How can you prepare parents for this step?
5. Do parents fully understand the entry process that you proposed at the time of enrollment? When parents are unable to spend much time with their child during the entry process, are you supportive and resourceful in helping them to do what they can?

Suggested Resources

Books and Articles

Balaban, Nancy. "The Role of the Child Care Professional in Caring for Infants, Toddlers, and Their Families," *Young Children,* Vol. 47 (July 1992), 66–71.

Addresses major elements of the caregiver's role, such as comforting a child, sharing knowledge of appropriate expectations, and facilitating parent-child separations.

Brazelton, T. Berry. *Working and Caring.* Boston, Mass.: Addison-Wesley Longman, 2000.

Explores the psychological issues of parents who choose child care for their infants and toddlers. Particularly useful are the sections on the steps in the developing parent-infant relationship and suggestions for choosing and adjusting to child care.

Gonzalez-Mena, Janet, and Nava Peshotan Bhavnagri. "Cultural Differences in Sleeping Practices: Helping Early Childhood Educators Understand," *Child Care Information Exchange,* Vol. 138 (March/April 2001), 91–93.

Focuses on how caregivers can provide developmentally and culturally appropriate care. Discusses the role of cultural values, beliefs, priorities, and goals and the importance of caregiver-parent communication to find creative solutions.

Gonzalez-Mena, Janet, and Nava Peshotan Bhavnagri. "Diversity and Infant/Toddler Caregiving," *Young Children,* Vol. 55 (September 2000), 31–35.

Suggests reflective dialogue to learn the cultural reasons for a family's different practices when one seeks creative solutions that satisfy both sides. Offers examples and ten questions to ask.

Leavitt, Robin L., and Brenda K. Eheart. *Toddler Day Care: A Guide to Responsive Caregiving.* Lexington, Mass.: Lexington Books, 1985.

A comprehensive guide to various developmental aspects of toddler caregiving. Excellent chapter on separation and working with parents.

Lerner, Claire, and Amy Laura Dombro. *Learning and Growing Together: Understanding and Supporting Your Child's Development.* Washington, D.C.: Zero to Three, 2000.

Offers four sections on how to support parents in their learning process: "How Parenthood Feels"; "Tuning In to Your Child"; "The Amazing First Three Years of Life"; "In Conclusion: Thoughts to Grow On."

McCracken, Janet Brown. *So Many Good-byes: Ways to Ease the Transition Between Home and Groups for Young Children.* Washington, D.C.: National Association for the Education of Young Children, 1995.

Brochure for parents on helping children adjust to a new child care program. Available from the National Association for the Education of Young Children, 1509 16th Street NW, Washington, DC 20036.

Osborne, Sandy. "Attachment and the Secondary Caregiver," *Day Care and Early Education,* Vol. 13, No. 3 (spring, 1986), 20–22.

Discusses the problems that separation anxiety in young children pose for the secondary caregiver. Offers strategies to facilitate separation from the parent or primary caregiver and to lessen the intensity of the child's anxiety response.

Phillips, Deborah A. "Infants and Child Care: The New Controversy," *Child Care Information Exchange,* Vol. 58 (November 1987), 19–22.

Argues that research does not support Belsky's position that infant child care for more than 20 hours per week is a risk factor for infants' insecure-avoidant attachment and children's maladaptive social behavior. Suggests that quality of care and family characteristics are major influences.

Provence, Sally, and others. *The Challenge of Daycare.* London and New Haven: Yale University Press, 1977.

Describes an infant/toddler service and research project, the Children's House. Shares clinically based information on caregiver-parent relationships, separation, appropriate curriculum, and nurturing environments for the young child. Contains practical information and forms to use for observations and curriculum planning.

Separation. Edited by Kathy Jarvis. Washington, D.C.: National Association for the Education of Young Children, 1987.

Clearly written and informative resource with beautiful photographs for child care personnel and parents about a neglected aspect of child care. Available from the National Association for the Education of Young Children, 1509 16th Street NW, Washington, DC 20036.

Stone, Jeannette Galambos. *Teacher-Parent Relationships*. Washington, D.C.: National Association for the Education of Young Children, 1987.

A compassionate booklet full of practical guidance and beautiful photographs. Focuses on a difficult but essential aspect of caregiving—a warm working relationship with parents. Available from the National Association for the Education of Young Children, 1509 16th Street NW, Washington, DC 20036.

Stonehouse, Ann, and Janet Gonzalez-Mena. "Working with a High-Maintenance Parent: Building Trust and Respect Through Communication," *Child Care Information Exchange*, Vol. 142 (November/December 2001), 57–59.

Describes how child care staff assisted one mother in working through separation difficulties with her eighteen-month-old. Emphasizes the value of empathy in helping staff members understand and support each family.

Viorst, Judith. *Necessary Losses*. New York: Simon & Schuster, 1998.

A compassionate, comprehensive discussion of the losses encountered from infancy to old age. The first section of the book is about infancy and childhood. The separation that must occur during the first two years of life is thus seen as part of a continuum and thereby gains more meaning. The cover has an appropriate definition of losses: "The loves, illusions, dependencies and impossible expectations that all of us have to give up in order to grow."

Audiovisuals

First Moves: Welcoming a Child to a New Caregiving Setting (First in the series, The Program for Infant/Toddler Caregivers, available in English, Spanish, and Chinese). Sacramento: California Department of Education, 1988. Video, 26 minutes.

This video demonstrates practical steps caregivers can take to help children be comfortable in a new setting, making those sometimes wrenching parent-child separations much easier for everyone. A child care video magazine, *First Moves: A Guide to the Video*, reviews the major concepts demonstrated in the video and develops other important points covered briefly by the visual presentation. Available from the California Department of Education, CDE Press, Sales Office, 1430 N Street, Suite 3207, Sacramento, CA 95814-5901.

Section Three:
Letting Families Know About You and Your Program

Caregivers are often more comfortable handling the complex problems and joys of a day spent with a group of very young children than they are trying to explain what they do and why. However, they do need to be prepared to answer the following questions: "What do you do with babies besides change their diapers?" "What can infants learn?" "How do I know my child will be safe?" "What do you do when one child hits another?" "Why aren't you teaching my toddler his letters and numbers?" "How soon will she be toilet trained?"

Communication About Your Program

Communicating the philosophy, goals, and practices of an infant/toddler program is an important part of the program itself. Start by thinking about your philosophy, policies, and practices and then put your thoughts in writing. In a program with more than one caregiver, this task can be a group endeavor. Writing down ideas helps to clarify thoughts and attitudes and ensures that all staff members have a common understanding of the program's approach to infant/toddler care.

Once you have discussed and written your ideas, you have the basis for creating written materials that you can share with parents. When you need to explain and discuss your positions on child care issues, you will be ready to use a combination of written and face-to-face communication. Here are some of the written, verbal, and nonverbal ways for communicating about the important issues of your program:

- Brochures
- Parent handbooks
- Informal conversations
- Parent conferences and meetings
- A positive program atmosphere

Brochures

One type of written communication is a brochure or flyer that briefly states the purpose and the special qualities of your program. Brochures can be given to prospective parents, people making casual inquiries, and community organizations to help publicize your program.

A brochure can be created with the help of a typewriter or word processor and a photocopy machine. Fold an 8-1/2 by 11-inch sheet of paper into three

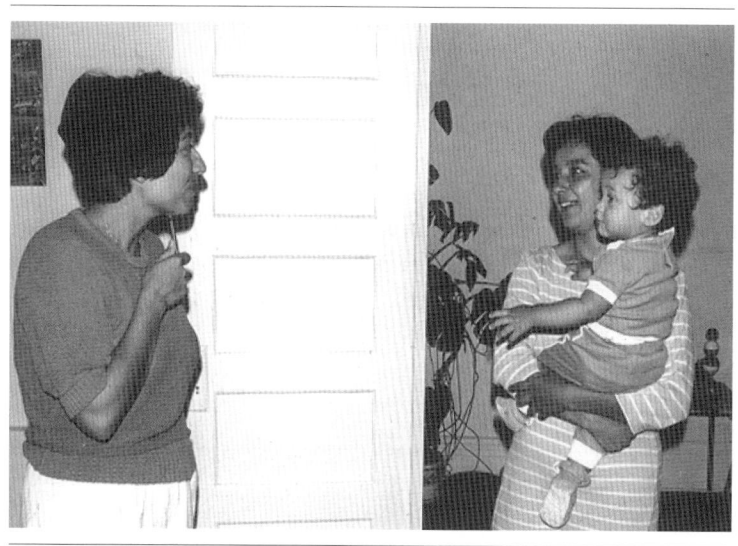

sections to give the brochure a more professional look. To make the brochure eye-catching, use photographs of children, children's artwork, or simple cutouts or drawings as illustrations. Keep the text short and easy to read. Include basic facts about the program, such as:

- Ages and number of children served
- The cost and eligibility requirements, if applicable
- Hours of operation
- Name, address, and telephone number of the program
- A brief statement about the program's philosophy of infant/toddler care
- Licensing information

Brochures are useful for introducing people to the program. They give people something to hold on to, to file for later use, or to pass on to a friend who is in need of the services offered. Brochures are not intended to tell parents all they need to know about the program if they want to enroll their child. For families who are seriously considering the program and for those in the process of enrolling, a parent's manual or handbook is essential.

Parent Handbooks

Parents entering a program need to have a written statement of its philosophy, policies, and practices. Although they will be hearing most of what they need to know in the initial enrollment interview, few parents will remember everything that is said. A parent's handbook will help prevent later misunderstandings and allow parents to read and think about the information on their own. A handbook also provides parents with a permanent record of what they can expect from the program and what is expected of them.

The parent's handbook may be as elaborate or as simple as you choose. For a family child care home and other small infant/toddler programs, the handbook can be brief because there is less information to impart. The number of caregivers is few, the organization is less complex, and parent participation is usually informal. A handbook may not even be needed. A one-page statement of policies may meet your needs.

Every program, however, will benefit from having written information for parents and staff that spells out the basic ideas guiding its daily operations. The following information should be included:

- Philosophy of care
- Admission and enrollment procedures
- Information about caregivers
- Emergency procedures
- Fee policies
- Parent involvement
- Program organization

Philosophy of Care

Your statement of philosophy can begin by affirming the role of the parent as the most important adult in the child's life. Explain how the partnership between parent and caregiver works. Let parents know staff members are available for questions, discussions, and just getting acquainted. Include a statement of the program's general goals, such as providing quality infant/toddler care in the community. Use the parent's handbook to communicate knowledge of how infants and toddlers learn.

A parent's handbook is a great way to:

1. Explain the value of a child care program appropriate to each child's age and development.
2. Discuss the importance of caregiving routines as learning experiences for infants and toddlers.
3. Describe your position on matters such as discipline, toilet learning,

and caregiver assignment to children.

Admission and Enrollment Procedures

Use this section to explain to parents exactly what will be expected of them during the entry process. Steps for admission into a program will usually include:

1. Pre-enrollment visits and interviews
2. Fulfillment of health requirements for child and parent
3. Completion of forms required by the program
4. Payment of the first month's fees, if any
5. Participation in the initial child-parent separation process

Information About Caregivers

In this section of the parent's handbook, write about the personal attributes, experience, and education of the caregivers in the program. Describe the qualifications sought when hiring new staff members. Other issues which can be discussed in this section are (1) the importance of staff stability in providing consistency of care; (2) the assignment of a primary caregiver; and (3) ratios of caregivers to children.

Emergency Procedures

Inform parents of the steps to prepare for emergencies, such as earthquakes, fires, floods, and so forth. The steps will include:

1. Maintaining emergency supplies of food, water, and flashlights
2. Practicing evacuation procedures on a regular basis
3. Keeping current information on where parents can be reached immediately in an emergency
4. Maintaining updated information on other adults who can take responsibility for each child in an emergency if the parent cannot be reached
5. Making arrangements for extended care of the children until everyone can be picked up

The handbook should also outline what steps are taken if a child is injured or becomes ill, when the family care provider or the child's primary caregiver cannot be there, or when a parent is unable to pick up the child on time.

Fee Policies

One section of the parent's handbook will deal with the handling of fees. Fee policies should clearly state:

1. How much fees are
2. Whether scholarships or fees on a sliding scale are available
3. When fees are due each month
4. Procedures taken when payments are late

Parental Involvement

Families need to know what kind and how much participation is expected of them in the program. In addition to the daily exchange of information and parent-caregiver conferences, other forms of involvement may include attending parent's meetings or working in the program with children.

The section on parental involvement is a good place to encourage parents to get to know other families in the program. Becoming acquainted with other families creates a sense of community that helps to strengthen feelings of security and connectedness among the children.

Program Organization

In a large program, the parent's handbook should include information about how the program is funded and how decisions are made. If the program's philosophy, policies, and procedures are mandated by funding sources or licensing requirements, make this clear. The organizational section of the manual should describe groups which create or influence program policy, such as a board of directors or parent council.

Informal Conversations

Written materials are only a starting point for the communication of important information and attitudes to incoming parents. In informal conversations, caregivers and parents will have the opportunity to discuss important child care issues in greater depth. Parents can ask questions. Caregivers can gain insights through listening, observing, and getting to know the child.

Listening is as important as talking.

During informal conversations with parents, you can facilitate communication in several ways. Allow parents to finish their sentences or the overly long anecdote. Keep eye contact and interject, "I see . . . , yes . . . , I know how you feel . . . you don't say!" Be ready to clarify your own point of view, as well. Parents may have different interpretations of written statements from what was intended, or they may feel that they disagree with something in the program's approach. When this happens, encourage open discussion, emphasizing the importance of the child's welfare to both the parents and the caregivers.

Parent's Conferences and Meetings

Parent's conferences and meetings are an excellent opportunity to express the program's philosophy of care and to hear the responses of parents. Whether conferences are regularly scheduled or specially arranged to address a particular issue, begin by restating the program's philosophy as it applies to the subject of the conference.

For example, in a parent's conference called to discuss a problem a child is having, begin by stating the importance of all areas of a child's development. Briefly bring the parent up to date on areas that are not a problem. The confer-

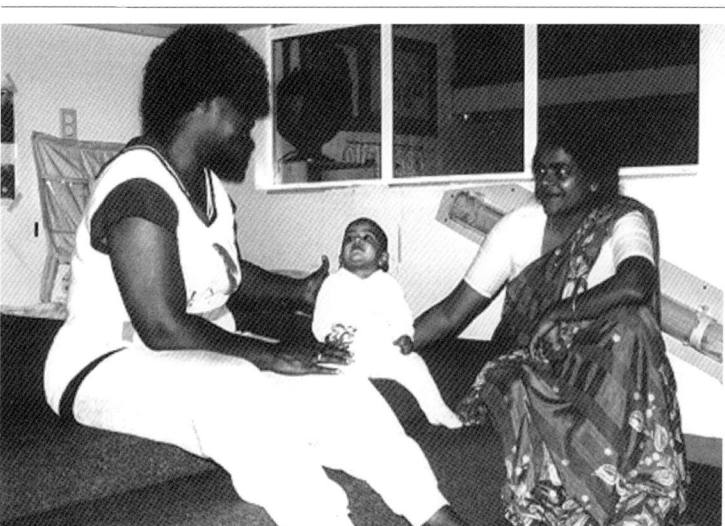

ence can then proceed to a discussion of the area in which the child is encountering difficulties, while maintaining a balanced perspective.

A Positive Program Atmosphere

When parents walk into a center or home for the first time, they immediately form impressions. They notice the following aspects of the setting:

1. Does it seem clean, orderly, and well-cared for?
2. Is it arranged so that infants and toddlers can enjoy the space and have both active and quiet play?
3. Does it provide comfortable seating for both adults and children?
4. Is it warm or cool enough, is there fresh air and light, and are the smells and sounds pleasant ones?
5. Do the adults as well as the children seem to be relaxed and enjoying themselves?

Thoughtful program managers and caregivers of infant/toddler programs recognize the impact of the emotional climate of the setting. They know they

First impressions are important.

need to work to maintain an atmosphere of openness, friendliness, and fairness. Family members can feel staff tension when problems are not handled in a professional manner.

Program managers can create a positive atmosphere with a visible commitment to the well-being of parents and staff members as well as the children. Providing opportunities for adults to learn and grow as well as expressing interest in each person are two ways of creating a positive atmosphere. Everyone involved in a child care program is important to each child's growth, including family members, caregivers, aides, secretaries, cooks, janitors, and bus drivers. Consideration and respect for each member of the "child care family" communicate a caring attitude that spreads throughout the program.

Points to Consider

1. Do you have written materials to give to incoming parents explaining the program's philosophy, policies, and procedures? How well do your materials represent your program? Do they need updating?
2. Are parents welcomed whenever they come to the child care setting? Do they feel free to arrive without calling first?
3. What are some ways you can encourage parents to take time for informal discussions of child care issues with caregivers?
4. How can you use parent meetings to deal with sensitive subjects with parents?

5. What are some ways to create a nurturing atmosphere for parents and staff, as well as the children in the program?

Suggested Resources

Books, Articles, and Pamphlets

Anderson, M. Parker. *Parent-Provider Partnerships: Families Matter.* Cambridge, Mass.: Harvard Family Research Project, 1998.

Advances the concept of family-centered child care by addressing the development of the child and family together. Offers family support principles that build on family strengths and the community's culture and resources.

Brazelton, T. Berry, and Stanley I. Greenspan. *The Irreducible Needs of Children: What Every Child Must Have to Grow, Learn, and Flourish.* Boulder, Colo.: Perseus Book Group, 2000.

Explores seven needs of infants and young children that, when met by families and professional caregivers, provide the fundamental building blocks for children's higher-level emotional, social, and intellectual abilities.

Bredekamp, Sue, and Carol Copple. *Developmentally Appropriate Practice in Early Childhood Programs* (Revised edition). Washington, D.C.: National Association for the Education of Young Children, 1997.

Provides comprehensive guidance for early childhood programs. Advocates the best practices for learning and development, including promoting creative discovery and cultural consistency.

Carter, Margie. "Communicating with Parents," *Child Care Information Exchange,* Vol. 110 (July/August 1996), 80–83.

Offers five strategies for enhancing communication, including keeping parents well informed; helping parents to introduce themselves in the classroom; and creating dialogue in newsletters and bulletins.

Carter, Margie. "Developing Meaningful Relationships with Families: Ideas for Training Staff," *Child Care Information Exchange*, Vol. 130 (November/December 1999), 63–65.

Presents strategies for improving relationships between child care providers and families, including creating family-friendly environments, rethinking parent meetings, and making memory books and videotapes.

Dodge, Diane Trister. "Sharing Your Program with Families," *Child Care Information Exchange*, Vol. 101 (1995), 7–11.

Offers guidelines for child care providers in working with parents to achieve mutual goals. Focuses on using the environment to express the philosophy and goals of the curriculum and establishing ongoing communication with families.

From Neurons to Neighborhoods: The Science of Early Childhood Development. Edited by Deborah A. Phillips and Jack Shonkoff. Washington, D.C.: National Academy Press, 2000.

Reports on an extensive review of scientific research and child policy centered on child development from birth to age five. Contains ten core concepts, including one that states: "Human development is shaped by a dynamic and continuous interaction between biology and experience."

Gonzalez-Mena, Janet, and Diane W. Eyer. *Infants, Toddlers, and Caregivers*. Columbus, Ohio: McGraw-Hill Higher Education, 2000.

Includes sections on parent-caregiver relationships, the nine-month separation in child care, and issues in providing culturally responsive care.

Nash, Margaret; Costella Tate; S. Gellert; and B. Donehoo. *Better Baby Care: A Book for Family Day Care Providers*. Washington, D.C.: The Children's Foundation, 1993.

Describes how babies grow, how they relate to others, how they think, common behaviors, nutrition, health, and safety. Includes section on how to prepare a home for child care, room by room. Available from The Children's Foundation, 725 15th Street NW, Suite 505, Washington, DC 20005.

Stone, Jeannette Galambos. *Teacher-Parent Relationships*. Washington, D.C.: National Association for the Education of Young Children, 1987.

A compassionate booklet full of practical guidance and beautiful photographs. Focuses on a difficult but essential aspect of caregiving—a warm working relationship with parents. Available from the National Association for the Education of Young Children, 1509 16th Street NW, Washington, DC 20036.

Audiovisuals

First Moves: Welcoming a Child to a New Caregiving Setting (First in the series, The Program for Infant/Toddler Caregivers, available in English, Spanish, and Chinese). Sacramento: California Department of Education, 1988. Video, 26 minutes.

This video demonstrates practical steps caregivers can take to help children be comfortable in a new setting, making those sometimes wrenching parent-child separations much easier for everyone. A child care video magazine, *First Moves: A Guide to the Video*, reviews the major concepts demonstrated in the video and develops other important points covered briefly by the visual presentation. Available from the California Department of Education, CDE Press, Sales Office, 1430 N Street, Suite 3207, Sacramento, CA 95814-5901.

Section Four:
Listening and Responding to Families

Many types of families seek child care. They include single-parent families headed by working mothers; fathers parenting alone; teenage parents living with their own parents; blended families consisting of couples with his, her, and their children; and two-career families in which both parents are equally involved in child rearing.

Families using child care may have recently arrived from other countries and speak little English. In addition, today's caregivers work with an increasing number of children at risk of neglect, abuse, illness, and extreme poverty. Many families are homeless or hungry, plagued with drug problems or AIDS. Whatever the family's situation, caregivers need to learn about the unique child-rearing practices and child care expectations of each family. Being open and responsive to the concerns of families in the program is one of the most important roles a caregiver can play.

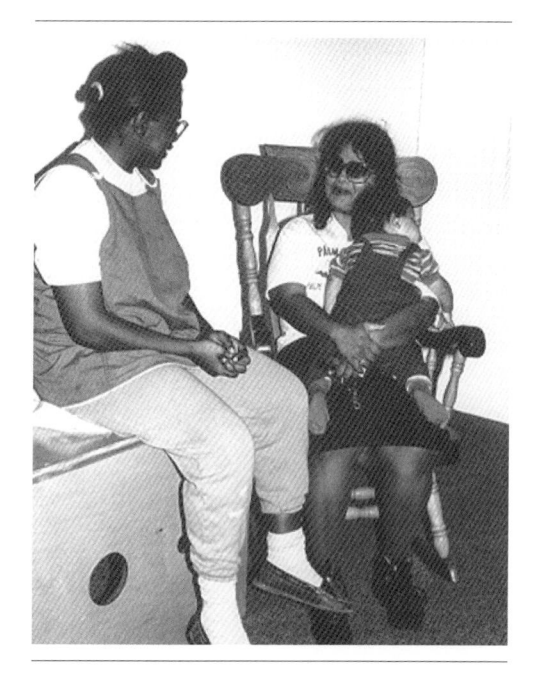

Listening to Parents

Because caregivers work with so many different types of families, clear communication is essential. This often takes skill and special thought. To begin, caregivers should spend more time listening than talking to parents. Listening is a more difficult and important art than talking; it consists of much more than just being quiet and not interrupting.

Active Listening

One proven listening technique is called *active listening*. In child care, a major part of active listening is paying attention to parent's messages—how parents expect their child to be treated and what they expect from you and from child care, in general.

Active listening is paying respectful attention to the parents' messages, both spoken and unspoken. Although these messages are not always communicated directly, they need to be listened to with great care and responded to with honesty and precision. A few active listening strategies follow.

Reading Body Language

Reading body language is an important part of active listening and can help you understand how the parent is feeling from day to day. The following situation is an example of how caregiver-parent communication can be improved by reading body language:

At the end of the day, the caregiver, Rosanne, and Robert's mother met as the mother arrived to pick up Robert.

ROSANNE: Robert seemed unusually fussy and irritable today. I wonder, is he coming down with something?

MOTHER: Oh, he is often like that at the end of the day. Are these Robert's clothes? I must hurry or I'll miss my bus.

After catching the bus, shopping for groceries, and cooking supper, Robert's mother finally felt how hot her child was and thought, *Why didn't Rosanne tell me Robert was ill?*

Rosanne was aware that Robert's mother had not really heard her, but by the time she realized she needed to say something more, Robert's mother had rushed out the door. If Rosanne had noticed the mother's body language as she came in (with a deep frown and an abrupt, quick stride), she would have realized that Robert's mother was in a hurry and wanted to leave the center as soon as possible. Quickly, Rosanne could have sized things up and said, "I have something important to tell you about Robert. I think he may be getting sick because he was so fussy, irritable, and tired." The rushed mother probably would have heard the words "something important" and "getting sick" and been more attentive to Rosanne's concerns.

Using Door Openers

The more parents talk, the more you can learn about them and their children. Parents are encouraged to talk when a caregiver shows genuine interest in what they have to say. Parents will not feel like talking if they are fairly sure the response will be a lecture or unsolicited advice.

Sometimes it is useful to employ "door openers" to draw parents out. These are phrases which invite parents to share their ideas and feelings or demonstrate interest in what the parent is saying. Examples of door openers are:

1. "I'd be interested in hearing your opinion."
2. "Interesting!"
3. "It sounds as if you have something to say about this."
4. "I've noticed that you...."
5. "Would you like to talk about it?"

These phrases encourage parents to continue, to elaborate, and to keep on talking. Door openers are especially effective when you and the parents are first getting to know each other and are

signals to parents that you really want to know what they think. Door openers reassure parents that they can talk safely without having a caregiver teach, advise, or lecture them.

Repeating What You Hear

You can test your listening skills and let a parent know the message has been heard simply by repeating in different words what the parent has said. This technique is especially effective with potentially controversial or sensitive subjects. The following example shows how this technique gives the caregiver time to come up with a thoughtful response to a parent's concern about her eighteen-month-old child:

>MOTHER: I wish the children had more big toys like wooden trucks and buses.

>CAREGIVER: Hmmm, you feel the children need more large wheel toys.

>MOTHER: Yes, I do. I think children need to be able to sit on wheel toys, push and pull them. Plastic doesn't give them the same sense of security.

>CAREGIVER: You're suggesting we invest in some wooden wheel toys big enough for toddlers to ride on?

>MOTHER: Yes, that's right.

As the conversation continued, the mother opened up and gave more details about what she wanted. The caregiver was able to think of how to meet the mother's concerns as she listened without interjecting her own opinions or arguments. The caregiver was not defensive.

>CAREGIVER: Perhaps we could organize a fund-raiser specifically for this purpose. Do you think you could help?

By suggesting an action which could be taken to meet the mother's concerns, the caregiver communicated that these concerns were valid. The mother agreed to the fund-raiser and began to make plans with other parents. The next time she had concerns, she felt more relaxed and flexible about them because she knew that the caregiver would listen and respond with respect.

Parents may become uneasy if their statements are merely repeated to them using the same words. Practice using this technique in a way that helps parents to expand their thoughts. Direct questioning also makes some parents feel uncomfortable or threatened. In such cases, other ways of getting information may be more effective, such as observation or using a door opener that invites a response.

First impressions are important.

Respecting Confidentiality

Although caregivers are not expected to be counselors to parents, they often find themselves in the role of empathetic listener to family concerns. Family members may confide personal concerns to you, trusting that you will understand their need for confidentiality. What should or should not be shared with co-workers is not always obvious. A good rule to remember is that sensitive information should never be shared with co-workers not directly involved in the problem, with members of other families, or with outside friends. Being able to size up what should be shared and what should be kept confidential is just another of the many challenges of caregiving.

Self-awareness in Relating with Others

Like everyone else, a caregiver is a person with a unique perspective, set of preferences, family circumstances, state of health, and family history. Take family history as an example of how personal experience influences caregiving. Throughout life, people carry with them the feelings acquired during their childhood. These feelings have a strong impact on human behavior when people become parents or caregivers. For example, a person who was accepted, supported, and loved in childhood is more likely to be accepting, supportive, and loving with an infant or toddler. On the other hand, someone whose childhood was unhappy, deprived, or harsh may tend to neglect, reject, or harshly punish a child. In order to be responsive to parents, you need to be aware of how your childhood influences the ways you think and behave.

The first step toward knowing yourself is to become aware of your personal feelings, values, and beliefs, especially as they affect the work of caring for infants and toddlers. These values and beliefs may stem from your own early childhood experiences. Consider your own childhood:

1. What you were like, how you felt, and how you were treated as a small child
2. What your family life was like, your relationship to your parents and siblings
3. Any crises, illnesses, divorce, death in the family, or move to a new place that put unusual stress on your family life
4. How you feel about your childhood now

Reach back for early memories and ask older family members what you were like. This information will give you another perspective on the attitudes and feelings which affect the way you care for children. You may discover why you are particularly attracted to certain infants and toddlers in your program. For example, a child may remind you of a favorite younger sibling or yourself when you were small. You may realize that what annoys you about a certain parent is that he or she reminds you of a disliked person from your childhood days.

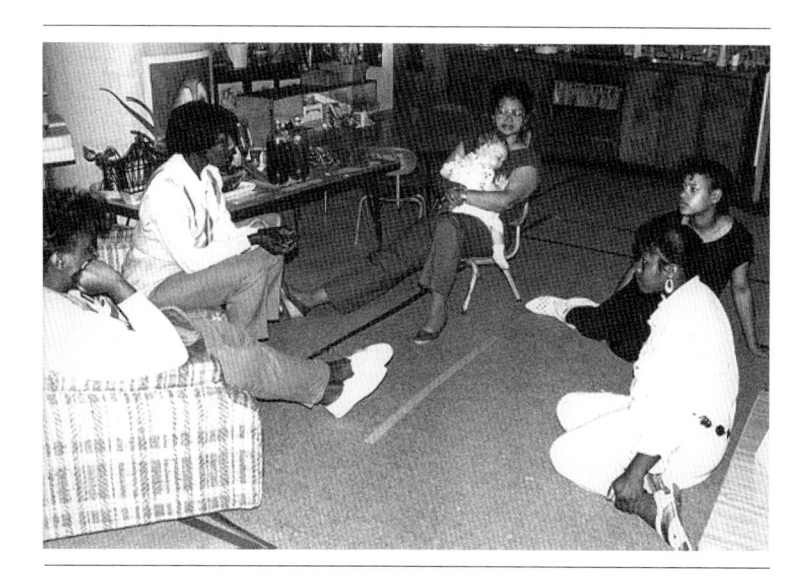

One way to understand how your childhood influences the way you relate to infants and their parents is to write down the things that you still resent or regret from your own childhood. You will find that these are almost always unresolved issues. Because these issues are unresolved for you, they can lead you to overemphasize them in your dealings with parents.

Being aware of how your past affects your present feelings can help you to understand better and empathize with the families in your program. For example, you may have the opportunity to tell one of your parents that you know how he or she feels about a certain family problem because your family went through the same difficult situation when you were a baby. This common experience can become the basis for a bond between you and that parent.

Now that you have considered how your past influences your attitudes, consider your present feelings and preferences. Spend some time thinking, writing, or talking with co-workers or friends about these issues:

- Your feelings as a caregiver
- Your likes and dislikes as an adult

Accepting Your Feelings About Caregiving

Maintaining the goodwill and energy to nurture caring partnerships with parents requires that caregivers also be sensitive to their own feelings about their work. Caregiving is not a 9-to-5 job. Situations will occur that require extra support for a family, such as when a parent's car breaks down and he or she cannot avoid being late picking up the child at the end of the day. Oftentimes, small but necessary tasks keep the caregiver from leaving work promptly.

At such times, it may be difficult to do what is needed without feeling angry, exploited, or just aggravated.

In order to handle all the demands on your time and energy, you need to:

1. Know your own limits. Be clear with parents about what these limits are, and you will less frequently find yourself in the position of giving too much.

2. Know when to stop "caring." Consistently taking home child care family troubles and problems of the day will lead to burnout and decrease your ability to be really helpful.

3. Be able to express your negative feelings to parents in tactful but straightforward terms.

As in all endeavors, caregivers must learn to live with partial success. Neither you nor the families and children you serve can be perfect. Having a friend to talk with can be a much-needed outlet for the intense work of caregiving. Talking with a friend can also help by providing you with another perspective on the many decisions that must be made.

Being a caregiver of very young children is not just a job; it requires deep personal involvement. Caregivers need maturity and the ability to deal cheerfully with things that make some people uncomfortable. Aspects of infant/toddler caregiving that can be unpleasant are:

1. Noise level
2. The feeling that the work is never done
3. Changing diapers, messy feedings
4. Fatigue
5. Emotional stress from enormous responsibility
6. Low pay, lack of status, and benefits

Caregivers may feel some resentment toward parents who place their children in infant/toddler care to return to jobs which pay much more than infant caregiving. Because caregiving involves performing tasks sometimes considered menial, such as changing diapers or cleaning up after meals, caregivers may feel sensitive about their status, especially around the working parents whom they serve. Occasionally, you may encounter parents who seem unaware of the high value of your work and your skills.

Sensitivity about the lack of status or resentment of the work and low pay can make it more difficult for you to practice active listening skills. You may sometimes find it hard to be as empathetic and caring as you need to be to support the growth of the parents and children you serve. Sensitivity about status can be less of a problem when you:

1. Actively work with other people concerned with child care issues to improve the status and pay of caregivers.
2. Take a relaxed moment to communicate these concerns to parents.
3. Maintain a sense of humor and perspective about the situation.

Sharing humor with parents brings out the lighthearted side of caregiving.

Knowing Your Likes and Dislikes

Everyone develops certain preferences and aversions in the process of growing into maturity. Sometimes preferences change; for example, children often dislike certain foods that they come to enjoy when they grow up. Other likes and dislikes remain throughout our lives. Lifelong preferences may even be associated with people as endearing aspects of their personalities. For example, a grandfather may be remembered for his way of eating six ears of corn on the cob at one time or an aunt for her many outfits in the color pink.

Let parents know you as an individual. You not only care for infants and toddlers but also have interests, preferences, and ties outside your professional life. Finding common interests with parents can make your work more enjoyable and also build the trusting partnership so important to the well-being of the children, the parents, and you.

Sharing likes and dislikes with parents, even insignificant ones, can also add a bit of humor to a situation. Suppose that you really dislike peas and have made that known to the parents in your program. You are serving peas to the children for lunch on a day a father is visiting with his toddler. He knows that you are too professional to let your dislike of peas influence the attitudes of your toddlers toward the wholesome vegetable. Through a raised eyebrow or other subtle way, the two of you now have an item to chuckle about as you cheerfully serve peas to the children.

Dealing with Prejudgments

Our expectations of situations and people are usually based on what we have learned in the past. Whether we acquire expectations from personal experiences, books and movies, or the opinions of relatives and friends, it is normal to use them to prejudge new experiences. Prejudging simply means forming attitudes and opinions before meeting a new person or situation.

Problems arise, however, when preconceived attitudes and opinions interfere with our seeing reality as it is. If prejudgments about people keep us from seeing them as they really are, then our treatment of those people may be inappropriate. For example, we may have the expectation that only boys will be interested in playing with trucks. As a result, we may fail to notice that a girl toddler is longingly eyeing a truck a boy toddler is playing with.

The first step in dealing with prejudgments is to be honest with yourself. Be open to the possibility that you may have expectations which affect your feelings about people. For example, so long as you say, "I don't judge people who use bad language," you have no way of examining your feelings and finding an appropriate way to handle them.

People who deny their prejudgments to themselves often come across as insincere. The parent who uses bad language may sense your disapproval without knowing what is causing it. You take the first step toward creating a better relationship with this person when you identify the source of your discomfort with him or her.

Even if you find it difficult to deal with the specific problem, you can realize that it is limited to one aspect of the person. Remember that you do have common interests—most notably the concern you share for the infant or toddler in your care.

Dealing with Differences

All of us have preferences about the way we like to live our lives and the way we want our children to live their lives. Sometimes these preferences are trivial and mean little to us while at other times they represent our core values. Life-style issues often create friction between a caregiver and a parent because one will be expected or asked to change the way he or she acts because of the desires of the other. What is needed when a child is placed in child care is a blending of styles so that both parent and caregiver come to feel that their core values are respected while negotiation takes place. Sometimes it is easy to come to agreement because a caregiver or parent will either see that doing things differently is not that serious or because he or she sees that doing it differently will actually support a core belief.

Relate with acceptance to the life-styles you encounter.

Try to be as flexible as possible with as many things as possible so that parents see that you take their wishes into consideration. Also, try to get to know parents well enough so that you understand when a life-style preference represents a core value they hold. Discuss with parents why they want you to do certain things, such as use cloth diapers, feed with certain types of foods, dress with specific clothing, and discipline in particular ways. Such talks will help you decide the best way to meet your needs and the parents' needs.

The following example illustrates how a caregiver might handle a sleep issue when he or she understands that the core values held by the parent and caregiver about the needs of the child are similar:

A teenage mother, Joyce, consistently brings in her toddler Tricia on Monday mornings so tired that the child is unable to stay awake through the morning until naptime.

Joyce is actually presenting a need to you. She needs help finding a way to balance the needs of her life-style with the developmental needs of her toddler. The first thing you can do is to invite Joyce to sit down and talk with you about Tricia's Monday morning fatigue. You recognize this as a sensitive subject, so setting a friendly, concerned tone is important.

"Tricia is doing great in child care," you may begin, "but on Mondays she is too tired to enjoy it. She often needs a nap earlier than the other toddlers so she ends up missing a lot." Then you ask, "Do you have any idea why Tricia is so tired after the weekend?"

Joyce may explain that because she is in high school she has to study every evening during the week. On weekend evenings, she enjoys playing music and socializing with her friends. Tricia is difficult to put to bed on those nights. She is attracted by the music and the company so Joyce lets her stay up until she falls asleep on her own.

You can ask, "Is there anything you could do differently so that Tricia will get more sleep?" Joyce may have some ideas of her own, or she may be able to illuminate the problem further. She probably does not want to give up her recreation time with her friends.

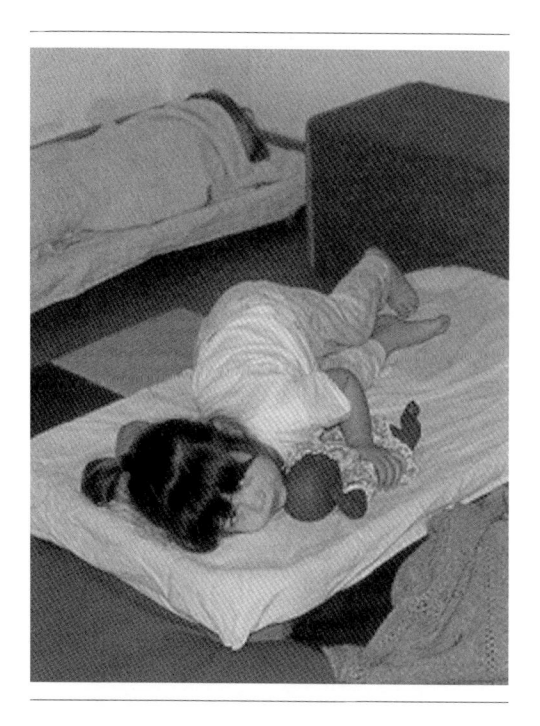

You can then offer some suggestions. Perhaps Tricia would be better off and Joyce herself could have more fun if Joyce told Tricia ahead of time that she could join Joyce and her friends for just a little while. Then it would be Tricia's "night-night time" and Joyce would take her to bed. Developing a ritual of saying good-night to each of Joyce's friends might ease the process. Turning down the music for a while would probably help Tricia to fall asleep more easily.

Paying careful attention to Joyce's responses during this process will give you valuable clues to what will really help her in this situation. From this session may come a change which will help Joyce to give better care for her child, or you may see, by reading Joyce's face, that your suggestion has not been accepted. You may need to wait a week or two and then try another approach.

Life-style differences often require special thought and handling on the part of the caregiver. Parents who do not want their toddlers to finger paint because the children might get paint on their clothing need both respect for their wishes and an explanation of the importance of messy play. Families who are vegetarians or have other strict rules regarding food and feeding of their child may hold different opinions than you do as to how mealtimes should be conducted. Babies who have become accustomed to being held most of the time and breast-fed frequently can be very demanding of your time, and you might believe that it would be better if they were handled differently. Nevertheless, these life-style differences must be respected and, when possible, program style altered to accommodate family preferences.

Sometimes the most difficult parents for caregivers to accept are those struggling the hardest to care for their families and those needing quality caregiving the most. You may sometimes feel resentful of or puzzled by parents' ways of doing things. Although it is usually easier to relate to people whose life-style is similar to one's own, caregivers need to develop and maintain cordial relationships with all the parents in their programs. When you view diverse values and behaviors as sources of interest and variety rather than as problems, you can create opportunities that enhance your relationships with parents whose life-styles differ from yours. Here are some things you can do:

1. Seek subjects of common interest to talk about.
2. Ask parents to tell you more about their ways of doing things.
3. Express your interest in and enjoyment of the infant or toddler.
4. Before bringing up issues with parents, think about and discuss your feelings and concerns with co-workers or friends.
5. Be tactful but direct in discussing what bothers you about a family's unusual ways of doing things and see whether you can negotiate a solution with the parents.

When caregivers relate only to parents whose values and life-styles are similar to theirs, caregivers can create many problems for themselves. The negative feelings of parents who are left out will make it more difficult to work with them and their children. These parents are likely to be less cooperative, and you may feel uncomfortable dealing with them.

A mother who received little love from her mother as an infant may find it difficult to show love toward her newborn baby, even though this love is one of the most important factors in a baby's development. Such parents may say things like, "Well, my father hit me when

I was bad and I turned out all right. I hit Thomas to teach him right from wrong." Or "I don't pick up Lisa when she cries because that will spoil her. I learned from my mom that crying won't get me anywhere. I don't want Lisa to be a crybaby."

Rather than give a parent general or offhand feedback, such as saying, "It would be good if you could be a little easier on Lisa," you might point out that infants need a good deal of picking up and holding; infancy is not a stage that lasts forever. Explain that infants whose needs for comfort and contact are usually met generally cry less and demand less attention as they grow, not more. Point out that research has shown such infants are often more able to handle things on their own when they get older. You might suggest that Lisa's mother try picking Lisa up for a specific period of time, perhaps one week, whenever she cries, and see how it feels.

Sometimes it is best to say nothing at first but to continue working to develop a comfortable relationship with the parent. The parent will be more open to your feedback if you have already established a friendly feeling between the two of you. Consider the following suggestions before you sit down to talk to a parent about his or her care of a child:

1. Create an opportunity to talk when you will not be interrupted and where you can set a relaxed tone to the conversation.
2. Be aware of how you use your voice as well as your words. Carefully chosen words expressed in a disapproving tone will put the parent off as much as a tactless statement of the problem.
3. Keep in mind the distinction between individual differences or cultural styles and inappropriate care. Remember that just because you do not like something does not make it wrong. You have your own childhood to deal with just as the parent does.
4. Ask the parent for his or her opinion about the child's behavior.
5. Finally, see if you can assist the parent in finding other ways of handling the situation.

Developing cordial relationships with families makes your job more satisfying

With adults, as with children, offering a positive alternative is the most effective way to change behavior. Attitudes and habits learned in childhood are not easily modified. Even when a parent would like to change a certain behavior toward the child, a stressful situation will tend to bring out the old pattern of response.

Remember, too, that another person's way of doing things may be just as valid as your way. The childhood experiences of parents can cause them to do things that sometimes seem irrational. Understanding the possible causes of parents' behavior can influence the ways you choose to help.

Caregivers sensitive to the challenges faced by parents often find that the support they offer to parents is deeply appreciated. Cultivate a positive relationship with every family in the group by really listening and responding as sensitively as possible. Even though developing cordial relationships takes time and energy, the effort will be worthwhile.

Common Sources of Tension

Common sources of tension that may bother caregivers are:

1. Parent being late in picking up the child
2. Parent putting food in the bottle
3. Parent forgetting to bring diapers
4. Parent insisting that child must not get dirty at the center
5. Family continually late with payments
6. Parent bringing in a child that he or she knows is ill
7. Parent expecting caregiver to be a parent to the parent
8. Parent bringing in child every Monday morning with diaper rash
9. Parent sending toys and food with child contrary to program policy
10. Parent refusing to put child's name on major clothing items because it is too much trouble

Common sources of tension that bother parents are:

1. Hearing nasty remarks about their child made by another parent
2. Caregiver acting as if he or she knows the child better than the parent
3. Child coming home with a new dress ruined by paint or with sand in hair
4. Child being bitten or hit often by another child or children
5. Finding child with a wet diaper at pickup time
6. Caregiver nagging parent about payment if it is only a few days late
7. Caregiver suggesting that the birthday cake be a simple sheet cake to avoid messiness
8. Caregiver expecting parent to sell tickets to make money for the child care program
9. Finding out that a caregiver has violated a confidence
10. Finding the child care facility messy

Points to Consider

1. How can you encourage parents to communicate? Do you make a point of listening more than talking? What makes listening "active"?
2. Do you take time to get to know parents as individuals? To let them know you?
3. How aware are you of your personal prejudices and preferences? How do these affect your relationships with parents?
4. How do you feel about your role as an infant/toddler caregiver? How do these feelings affect your ability to hear and respond to parents' concerns? What steps can you take to become more comfortable in your relationships with parents?
5. What are some of the differences in life-styles among families in your infant/toddler care program? How do you feel about the differences? Are there steps you can take to negotiate uncomfortable differences?

Suggested Resources

Books, Articles, and Pamphlets

Carter, Margie. "Communicating with Parents," *Child Care Information Exchange,* Vol. 110 (July/August 1996), 80–83.

Offers five strategies for enhancing communication, including keeping parents well informed; helping parents to introduce themselves in the classroom; and creating dialogue in newsletters and bulletins.

Dittmann, Laura. "Where Have All the Mothers Gone?" in *Infants: Their Social Environments*. Edited by Bernice Weissbourd and Judith S.

Musick. Washington, D.C.: National Association for the Education of Young Children, 1981.

Important insights for caregivers on working mothers.

Dodge, Diane Trister. "Sharing Your Program with Families," *Child Care Information Exchange*, Vol. 101 (1995), 7–11.

Offers guidelines for child care providers in working with parents to achieve mutual goals. Focuses on using the environment to express the philosophy and goals of the curriculum and establishing ongoing communication with families.

Fisher, Roger, and William Ury. *Getting to Yes: Negotiating Agreement Without Giving In* (Second edition). New York: Penguin Publishing, 1991.

Offers a concise, step-by-step strategy for coming to mutually acceptable agreements. Based on studies and conferences conducted by the Harvard Negotiation Project, a group that deals with all levels of conflict resolution.

Galinsky, Ellen. *The Six Stages of Parenthood*. Reading, Mass.: Addison-Wesley Longman, 2000.

Based on interviews with a broad cross-section of American families, the book discusses various stages of parenting which require different skills.

Gonzalez-Mena, Janet, and Dianne W. Eyer. *Infants, Toddlers, and Caregivers*. Mountain View, Calif.: Mayfield Publishing Co., 2001.

This expanded edition includes sections on parent-caregiver relationships and nine-month separation in child care and multicultural situations.

Gonzalez-Mena, Janet, and Nava Peshotan Bhavnagri. "Diversity and Infant/Toddler Caregiving," *Young Children,* Vol. 55 (September 2000), 31–35.

Suggests reflective dialogue to learn the cultural reasons for a family's different practices when one seeks creative solutions that satisfy both sides. Offers examples and ten questions to ask.

Leavitt, Robin Lynn, and Brenda Krause Eheart. *Toddler Day Care: A Guide to Responsive Caregiving*. Lexington, Mass.: Lexington Books, 1985.

Provides a comprehensive guide to various developmental aspects of caring for toddlers. Includes a chapter on separation and working with parents.

Miller, Karen. "Caring for the Little Ones—Developing a Collaborative Relationship with Parents," *Child Care Information Exchange*, Vol. 135 (September/October 2000), 86–88.

Discusses the benefits of collaborative relationships with parents and provides suggestions for developing rapport and offering support.

Modigliani, Kathy. *Parents Speak About Child Care* (Second edition). Boston, Mass.: Wheelock College Family Child Care Project, 1997.

Examines parent and family attitudes through 23 focus group discussions of parents' child care experiences in nine U.S. cities. Analyzes videotapes resulting from the project.

O'Brien, Marion. *Inclusive Child Care for Infants and Toddlers: Meeting Individual and Special Needs*. Baltimore, Md.: Paul H. Brookes Publishing Company, 1997.

Provides a resource for infant/toddler caregivers in inclusive settings and a training guide for students and beginning teachers. Chapter 3 deals with parents as partners and suggests ways in which to communicate with and involve family members in their children's care.

Schweikert, Gigi. "I Confess, I've Changed—Confessions of a Child Care Provider and a Parent," *Child Care Information Exchange*, Vol. 111 (September/October 1996), 90–92.

Explores challenges in the communication between child care providers and parents through the eyes of a child care educator who is also a parent.

Schweikert, Gigi. "Remember Me? I'm the Other Parent—Insights for Meeting the Needs of Both Parents," *Child Care Information Exchange,* Vol. 126 (March/April 1999), 14–17.

Presents tips for meeting the needs of parents who are unable to see their children's teachers regularly. Focuses on the importance of providing accurate information and relying on various methods of communication.

Stanley, Diane. "How to Defuse an Angry Parent," *Child Care Information Exchange,* Vol. 108 (March/April 1996), 34–35.

Offers a four-step plan for defusing a parent's anger: listen carefully; make sure the problem is well understood; acknowledge the parent's feelings; and explain the plan of action.

Stonehouse, Anne, and Janet Gonzalez-Mena. "Working with a High-Maintenance Parent: Building Trust and Respect Through Communication," *Child Care Information Exchange*, Vol. 142 (November/December 2001), 7–59.

Describes how child care staff assisted one mother in working through separation difficulties with her eighteen-month-old. Emphasizes the value of empathy in helping staff members understand and support each family.

Sturm, Connie. "Creating Parent-Teacher Dialogue: Intercultural Communication in Child Care," *Young Children*, Vol. 52 (July 1997), 34–38.

Highlights the Parent-Teacher Dialogue Project (San Francisco Bay Area) to encourage open dialogue between parents and caregivers.

Section Five:
Considering the Family in Its Culture

Every parent, child, and caregiver has feelings, perceptions, and behavior that come from living in a particular culture. Cultural values and practices are passed down from one generation to the next, mainly through the process of child rearing. In the United States, a wide range of cultural traditions is represented. Many infant and toddler caregivers today have the difficult but exciting task of relating to parents and children from various cultures. In order to provide appropriate care, caregivers need to understand how the families enrolled in their programs are affected by their cultural backgrounds.

Establishing Communication

An attitude of acceptance and support is the key to successful partnerships between caregivers and parents from different cultures. For such a partnership to occur, communication is essential. Therefore, the first step is to find out whether you and the parent speak the same language. If not, find out whether there is a caregiver or staff member who speaks the family's language.

When there is no one available in the program who speaks the family's language, there may be an adult in the family with whom you can exchange important information. If there is not, use an outside interpreter at first. As soon as possible, however, every effort should be made to expand staff to include caregivers who are from the cultures of the families served or who at least speak their language. The ability to communicate with family members is critical to a positive child care experience for all.

Even when both the caregiver and the parent speak English, keep in mind that some words or phrases may not mean the same to each of them. Many cultures and subcultures flourish among English-speaking people. To ensure mutual understanding, use the active listening and repeating techniques described in Section Four.

Different Cultures

One way to develop good relationships with people from different cultures is to show an interest in their cultures. When you actively listen and ask parents questions, you show your interest in their customs and attitudes. You express

43

respect by inviting families to bring special foods, crafts, rituals, songs, and stories to the program. People from different cultures do things differently, and their customs can be a source of enrichment and enjoyment for caregivers, parents, and children alike.

Even more important is learning about how people from different cultures feel the values and rules of their culture should be transmitted to infants and toddlers. How are issues such as individuality, responsibility, respect, and physical and verbal expression regarded? How are young children responded to, addressed, or considered? These issues should be topics of conversation between you and the parents.

Families from Difficult Circumstances

When dealing with recent arrivals from poor or war-torn countries or those who have been subjected to urban or rural poverty in this country, you have a tremendous opportunity. You can make a difference in the way these families see themselves in the context of the dominant culture, and in what they will communicate to their infants and toddlers. Dealing with such families requires sensitivity and genuine concern.

As these families begin to develop relationships with you, they may share personal information about themselves and the circumstances under which they arrived in this country. This information should not be sought from them and, if offered, should be treated as confidential.

Child care may be the first or one of few voluntary contacts a family has with the surrounding community. The feelings developed about the child care program are likely to set the tone for trust or lack of trust in other community services. If the family and its culture are treated with warmth and respect, the adjustment to the dominant culture, as well as to child care, will be enhanced.

Supporting Cultural Diversity

Although people of many different cultures have arrived in the United States in recent years, cultural diversity has been a part of American history since its beginning. Native American culture predates northern European culture in this country by hundreds of years, and African Americans have been here for more than three centuries. People from every continent have made the United States their home, each group bringing its own cultural heritage.

Here are some ways you can help families from different cultural heritages, both long-time Americans and recent arrivals, feel at home:

1. Create an environment that reflects the cultures of the families in the program. For example, a toddlers' housekeeping corner might have chopsticks, ethnic dolls, and doll clothes, as well as spoons, clothes,

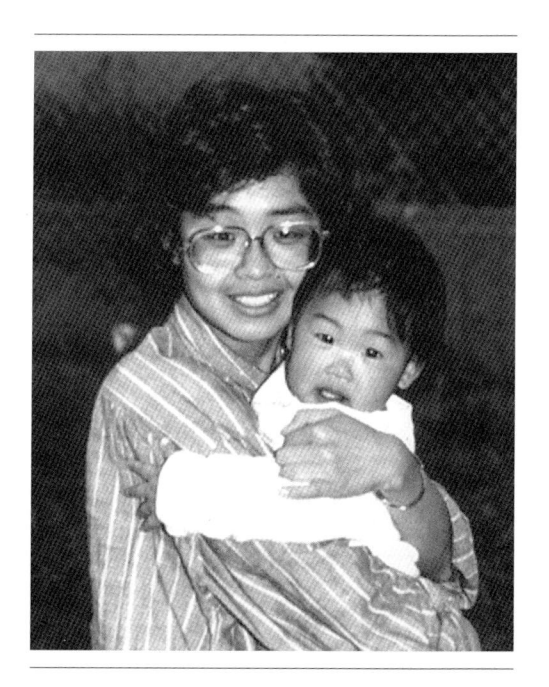

and hats from different cultures for boys and girls to dress up in.

2. Involve family members by inviting them to share their skills. Perhaps one of the grandparents plays a traditional instrument. An aunt might bring baskets or stitchery and demonstrate how these products are made.

3. Include art, music, and photographs from cultures represented in the program. Make sure the families see images similar to their own culture in the child care setting.

4. Find out what language is spoken at home. Try to learn a few common words in the foreign language, such as hello and good-bye, thank you, family, baby, diaper, bottle, eat, hungry, apple, cracker, milk, happy, sad, and so on.

5. At storytimes, have staff tell stories, and folk tales from various cultures. Ask parents to teach you a lullaby or a favorite nursery rhyme in their language.

When the caregiver and the family come from different cultures, the need to respect and accept different cultural practices becomes critical. Customs practiced by one may seem strange to the other, especially if it is the first time that such cultural differences are encountered. Yet the partnership between the primary caregiver and family members from a different culture is particularly important. Without it, the child will not receive the consistency of care he or she needs to learn and grow.

Certain cultural differences are more likely than others to become issues in child care situations. The following types of differences may raise issues:

- Values
- Roles of family members

Multicultural experiences can be enriching for caregivers, parents, and children.

- Discipline of children
- Self-care
- Routines
- Religious beliefs and rituals
- Attitudes toward property
- Health practices

Learning about these differences from the families can be useful if you keep in mind that they do not necessarily apply to everyone or every subculture within a culture. For example, it is important not to lump together all cultures from a certain region, such as Korean, Japanese, and Chinese. Each culture has its own customs, language, and common experience.

Values

Although there are many subcultures in the United States today, one major set of values and expectations can be identified as the dominant culture. This culture fosters the development of children who are outgoing, friendly, informal, individualistic, explorative, and vocal about their feelings. Japanese culture, on the other hand, teaches young children to be more reserved and to maintain harmony in the family. Group achievement, rather than personal excellence, is emphasized.

Other cultures, such as Chinese, Hawaiian, and Native American, also emphasize cooperation rather than individual success and competition. Loyalty to the family and respect for one's elders are most important.[1]

---

[1] Margie K. Kitano, "Early Education for Asian American Children," *Young Children,* Vol. 35 (January 1980), 13–24.

In Hispanic culture, maintaining *la dignidad,* honor or a good reputation, is very important. *Respeto* (respect) is shown by a pattern of ceremonial politeness observed by all but the closest relatives and friends.[2] Telling a Hispanic mother something negative about her child may be interpreted as an assault on her *dignidad.* Learning about a family's values is the key to good caregiver-parent relations.

Roles of Family Members

How families are structured and managed is usually culturally determined. For example, traditional Hispanic and Southeast Asian families are headed by a male member who makes all the important decisions.

Here is an example of how a caregiver's lack of awareness of family structure can cause a misunderstanding between the caregiver and parent:

> Kim is a Korean two-year-old who likes to wander. The caregiver is anxious that he may not be safe as he fails to respond when she goes after him. She reported this to Kim's mother.
>
> CAREGIVER: You know, I'm worried about Kim. He wanders off and when I go after him, he runs away. I'm afraid he will get hurt.
>
> MOTHER: I will take care of it.

The mother's way of taking care of it was to tell her husband. Since he had not had the opportunity to speak directly to the caregiver, he believed it was his responsibility to improve Kim's behavior with punishment and a lecture about the shame Kim was bringing to the family.

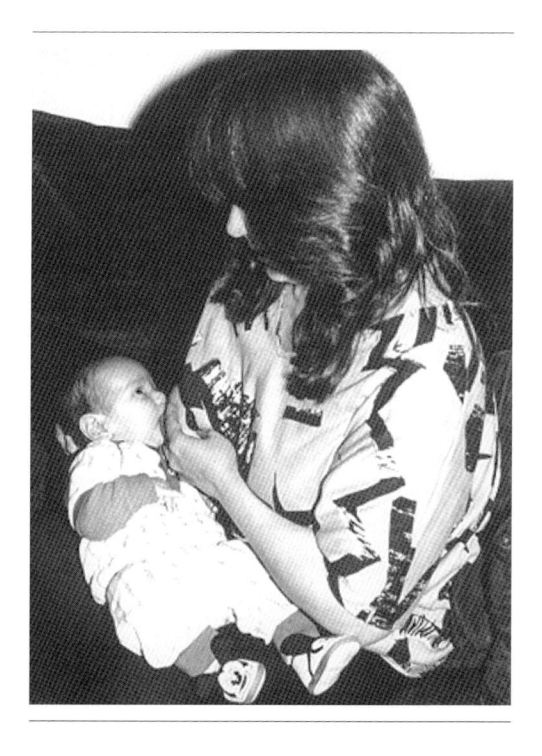

[2]Ruby R. Leavitt, *The Puerto Ricans: Culture Change and Language Deviance,* Tucson, Ariz.: University of Arizona Press, 1974, p. 46.

This was not the outcome the caregiver was seeking. An awareness of different family structures on the part of the caregiver in this situation might have led her to frame the problem differently, include the father in the original discussion of Kim's problem and, ultimately, to foster a different outcome.

Discipline of Children

When, by whom, and how children are disciplined in families reflect the family's structure and value system. Many cultures allow children a long time to grow into responsibility for actions. Parents in some cultures seldom punish children before the age of five. When young children are disciplined, methods used may be gentle and persuasive. For example, the Hopi mother says in a soft voice, "No, no, that is not the Hopi way," as she gently withdraws the child's hand from something he or she must not touch.

In some cultures, the responsibility for the discipline of young children is shared by the mother and father, while in other cultures it falls to the male head of the household. In the Hopi culture, for example, the disciplinarian is the mother's brother. How you socialize a child is always important and should be a part of parent-caregiver conversations.

Self-care

In many cultures infants and toddlers are not expected to learn self-care as early as in American culture. And in some cultures the infant or toddler is considered a part of the mother who carries the child on her back wherever she goes. A child may not be weaned from the breast until another child comes along. When the emerging toddler is displaced from his or her mother's back by a younger sibling, the adults and older children often share responsibility for that toddler's care and safety.

Toilet learning for young children is not considered important in every culture. Babies are not always kept in diapers. If weather permits, the child wears only a shirt and is allowed to go outside and eliminate when necessary. Cleanliness, especially to the degree required in infant and toddler care settings, is less important in some traditional cultures. Parent-caregiver misunderstandings can arise from issues about self-care.

Routines

In many cultures, families include infants and toddlers in their activities. The idea of having an outsider "baby-sit" while the parents go out for the evening is foreign to them. Also, in other cultures infants often sleep with their mothers. Family routines naturally accommodate infants' needs so that it is unnecessary to have specific routines. When the infant or toddler gets sleepy, he or she finds a cozy corner to curl up in and goes to sleep.

Feeding practices for infants and toddlers vary from culture to culture. For example, weaning and the introduction of solid foods are two areas in which these differences are often reflected.

Caregivers need to be open to different ways of meeting infants' and toddlers' needs. In the context of the child's family and culture, such practices may be most appropriate and supportive of the child's growth. Child care practices may need to be modified to be as consistent as possible with routines at home, rather than the reverse.

Religious Beliefs and Rituals

In providing care to families of various cultures, caregivers will encounter religious practices very different from their own. Crops may have been planted and harvested according to religious beliefs or occurrences in nature, such as a full moon. In certain cultures, ritualistic dances and ceremonies may accompany every special family occasion.

With families of the Moslem, Hindu, Buddist, Christian, and Jewish religions, as well as other religions, uneven attendance in the child care program may result from the observance of religious holidays. The observance of some holidays may last as long as a week. For instance, some Mexican families return to Mexico for an extended Christmas holiday of four to six weeks.

Attitudes Toward Property

Some cultures do not recognize individual property. Possessions belong to all. A recognized method is used to dispense what is needed to family members. Problems in child care may arise because small toys may be taken home by children or parents who assume that they are community property. Caregivers who understand the meaning of this behavior can remain calm and do some preventive planning.

Health Practices

Caregivers have a great deal of responsibility for the health of the children in their care. You may be legally bound to meet such requirements as tuberculosis tests, physical examinations, and vaccinations. In addition, you may have other responsibilities related to hygiene, nutrition, or referral to medical treatment for illness. Some of these requirements and practices may be difficult for families from other cultures to understand or accept. If you are somewhat familiar with the cultures of these families, you can handle these situations with sensitivity.

One potential problem is that drawing blood, even for a medical examination, is frowned on in many cultures. If a blood test is legally required, the male head of the family may have to give his consent. In addition, recently arrived immigrants may be fearful of hospitals and the medical profession in general. They may hesitate to sign a permission slip to call an ambulance in case of an emergency.

Many refugee families will have had extensive physical examinations before being allowed to enter the U.S. The results of tuberculosis tests required for enrollment in child care may be positive due to previous medical procedures. When working with refugee families, find out the type, extent, and dates of tests done by the government.

Finally, some cultures rely on rituals for curing illness, while others use herbs. To caregivers, these customs may endanger the child; however, for the families involved they are a way of maintaining faith with the ways of their past. They believe their practices work; they are not so sure about modern methods.

In such cases, the following actions may be needed to resolve these problems:

1. Be very clear about what you believe the child needs while remaining open to the feelings of the family and respectful of their beliefs.
2. Bring in a medical professional from the same culture to work with the family.
3. Contact community resources for support.

Family associations and social service agencies in areas with large immigrant and refugee populations are often available to assist recently arrived families in making the transition to life in the United States.

Discomfort About Differences

It is common for people to feel threatened by others who are different from them. When caregivers and the families they serve come from different racial or cultural backgrounds, they may have feelings which, at least initially, make it difficult for them to treat each other with empathy and respect. The first step toward solving this problem can be taken by "walking in the other's shoes." The second step is to recognize that developing mutual trust may take longer between people who are culturally or racially different, but that trust will usually develop in an atmosphere of consistent acceptance, fairness, and goodwill. The third step is to take the risk of recognizing unexpressed feelings and bring them out into the open. The fourth step is to realize that one can never learn all there is to know about a culture. A sense of being ill at ease is normal. Try to learn more but do not expect to know everything about another culture. The rewards of this kind of openness will be a harmonious child care program in a lively atmosphere of cultural exchange.

Differences Within a Culture

Not all families within a culture are the same. Just as attitudes, customs, and child-rearing practices vary among families of the dominant American culture, there are tremendous variations between families of the same foreign culture. Some families adapt much more quickly than others. Some carry with them bitter memories and traumatic losses which influence their daily lives.

> *Each family is a culture in itself, and each person in it a unique individual.*

Variations between one family and another of the same culture are often greater than between two families of different cultures. Here is an illustration:

A group of ten Eritrean refugee families came into a program at the same time. Seven were from an isolated rural area and were illiterate in their own language. The other three were from an urban area, knew their own language well, and had an elementary knowledge of English.

Five of the women were Moslem; the other five were Christian. All but one dressed in native dress—flat shoes, long skirts, and white voile fabric draped around their heads and waists. One wore tight jeans and high heels and used make-up.

Many of these differences were superficial, but the temperaments and interests of the women also varied. Two were very lethargic, four were quick learners, and one seemed indifferent. One was an excellent cook and enjoyed sharing her food with the other Eritreans and caregivers. Three were eager to learn about using the electric sewing machines.

To treat each of these women alike or to expect the same kind of behavior from all ten of them would have been

respect each other as individuals, transcending and eliminating barriers based on race, sex, or ability. Available from the National Association for the Education of Young Children, 1509 16th Street NW, Washington, DC 20036.

Duffy, Roslyn, and others. "Parent Conferences: Beginnings Workshop," *Child Care Information Exchange*, Vol. 116 (July/August 1997), 39–58.

Presents six workshop sessions on parent conferences. Chapter 3 focuses on meeting with parents of infants. Chapter 6 addresses working with non-English-speaking families.

Fisher, Roger, and William Ury. *Getting to Yes: Negotiating Agreement Without Giving In* (Second edition). New York: Penguin Publishing, 1991.

Offers a concise, step-by-step strategy for coming to mutually acceptable agreements. Based on studies and conferences conducted by the Harvard Negotiation Project, a group that deals with all levels of conflict resolution.

Gonzalez-Mena, Janet. *Multicultural Issues in Child Care* (Third edition). Mountain View, Calif.: McGraw-Hill Higher Education, 2000.

Based on respect for cultural pluralism, this concise text is designed to increase caregiver sensitivity to different cultural practices and values. The text references numerous research studies.

Gonzalez-Mena, Janet. "Resolving Disagreements," *Coordinate* (1992), 12–14.

Presents strategies for resolving cultural conflicts through understanding and negotiation, caregiver education, parent education, and conflict management.

Gonzalez-Mena, Janet. "Taking a Culturally Sensitive Approach in Infant/Toddler Programs," *Young Children*, Vol. 47 (January 1992), 4–9.

Offers help for caregivers to improve their sensitivity to cultural and individual differences and increase communication. The principles include strategies such as becoming clear about one's own values and goals and using a problem-solving rather than a power approach to conflicts.

Gonzalez-Mena, Janet, and Dianne W. Eyer. *Infants, Toddlers, and Caregivers*. Mountain View, Calif.: Mayfield Publishing Co., 2001.

This expanded edition includes sections on parent-caregiver relationships and nine-month separation in child care and multicultural situations.

Gonzalez-Mena, Janet, and Nava Peshotan Bhavnagri. "Cultural Differences in Sleeping Practices: Helping Early Childhood Educators Understand," *Child Care Information Exchange*, Vol. 138 (March/April 2001), 91–93.

Focuses on how caregivers can provide developmentally and culturally appropriate care. Discusses the role of cultural values, beliefs, priorities, and goals and the importance of caregiver-parent communication to find creative solutions.

Gonzalez-Mena, Janet, and Nava Peshotan Bhavnagri. "Diversity and Infant/Toddler Caregiving," *Young Children*, Vol. 55 (September 2000), 31–35.

Suggests reflective dialogue to learn the cultural reasons for a family's different practices when one seeks creative solutions that satisfy both sides. Offers examples and ten questions to ask.

Infant/Toddler Caregiving: A Guide to Culturally Sensitive Care. Edited by Peter L. Mangione. Sacramento: California Department of Education, 1995.

This guide is written to help infant/toddler caregivers become more culturally sensitive. It is intended to help caregivers (1) improve their understanding of themselves and discover how they are influenced by their own cultural beliefs; (2) improve their understanding of the children and families they serve; and (3) learn to relate to cultural issues and thereby become more effective caregivers.

Lynch, Eleanor W., and Marci J. Hanson. *A Guide for Working with Children and Their Families: Developing Cross-Cultural Competence* (Second edition). Baltimore, Md.: Paul H. Brookes, 1998.

Offers practical advice for working with children and families of diverse heritages. Includes new examples and helpful appendixes explaining culturally diverse courtesies, customs, events, practices, and vocabulary.

National Black Child Development Institute publications include a newsletter and calendar featuring issues and important dates in history relevant to the development of black children.

Available from the National Black Child Development Institute, 1463 Rhode Island Ave. NW, Washington, DC 20005; telephone (202) 387-1281.

Schorr, Lizbeth B., and Daniel Schorr. *Within Our Reach: Breaking the Cycle of Disadvantage and Despair.* New York: Doubleday and Co., 1988.

Reviews intervention programs created over the past 20 years for young children at risk. Maintains that the nation already has the answers for providing appropriate educational intervention and support and does not need to reinvent strategies or approaches. Describes various methods of working with difficult issues and dysfunctional families.

Sturm, Connie. "Creating Parent-Teacher Dialogue: Intercultural Communication in Child Care," *Young Children*, Vol. 52 (July 1997), 34–38.

Highlights the Parent-Teacher Dialogue Project (San Francisco Bay Area) to encourage open dialogue between parents and caregivers.

Audiovisuals

Culturally Diverse Families. New York: Young Adult Institute, 1987. Video, 28 minutes.

Three professionals talk about approaches that help sensitize caregivers working with culturally diverse families. Includes training guides for instructor and staff. Available from the Young Adult Institute, 460 W. 34th St., New York, NY 10001; telephone (212) 563-7474.

Essential Connections: Ten Keys to Culturally Sensitive Child Care. Sacramento: California Department of Education, 1993. Video, 36 minutes.

Explores the meaning of culture in the lives of young children and the role of culture in the development of a child's self-esteem. It emphasizes the importance of providing culturally consistent care in child-care settings and learning about the child's home through the family. A video magazine is included.

Section Six:
Involving Parents in the Program

Many programs have difficulty getting parents involved. Caregivers may be reluctant even to broach the subject to the families they serve. They may feel that parents are too busy or not interested, or that they themselves have inadequate leadership skills. In fact, caregivers in both centers and homes have a great deal to share with the parents in their programs. Parent involvement does not have to be formal. After all, the goal is to establish a caregiver-family-child bond.

Setting the Stage for Parent Involvement

To involve parents in a child care program, pay attention to their particular circumstances and needs. Parent involvement policies and strategies need to fit the families enrolled—to adapt to changing family patterns and the cultural makeup of the group.

Few families today represent the kind of family for whom earlier parent participation programs were designed. For example, nowadays a majority of families seek full day care for their children. Although the need for a strong parent-caregiver relationship is great, so are the other demands on parents' time.

Avoid the unrealistic position that everyone must contribute X number of hours unless such participation is mandated by a funding agency. If mandates exist, be specific and straightforward with families from the start. Make certain parents understand what is required.

Life-styles and cultural trends have also changed in recent years. Many programs serve refugee and immigrant families as well as families living in nontraditional groups. Certain parent participation activities may not be valued in a particular culture or may carry negative connotations of caste or class. The roles of family members may differ from the dominant American culture. Families need options that fit their specific circumstances if they are to become involved in their child's care.

Getting parents to spend time in activities related to child care in addition to dropping off and picking up their children has always been a challenge. The family time of those who use child care is often stretched thin by demands of work or study, home management, and child rearing. To get parents involved, you will need to create an atmosphere of acceptance and responsiveness to their needs. Opportunities for participation need to be appealing and meaningful so that parents feel they are missing something important if they are not involved.

Encourage Feelings of Partnership

Remind parents that quality care of infants and toddlers can result only from a caring partnership between parents and caregivers. Speak of "our" program, not "my" program. Use words like "our" and "we" to show that you want to include parents, that you really do consider them an important part of child care. For example, ask, "How do you think we can work together to give Lisa a good life here and at home?" By listening carefully to the parent's response, you show your commitment to the child and to the partnership.

Help Parents Feel at Home

Parents sometimes feel uncomfortable in the child care setting. They may fear that they are intruding. A smile, a friendly greeting, or a cup of coffee can reassure them that they are welcome. Create a special place for parents by displaying attractive posters and interesting books and articles about relevant child-rearing issues. When parents see that the child care site is a place for them as well as their infants or toddlers, they will feel freer to become involved, to ask questions, and to offer help.

Establishing the feeling of involvement will take time. As in other relationships, there is a period of getting to know one another. The seed is planted when the parent is made to feel welcome. As trust develops and grows, the relationship takes root.

Parent Involvement in Center and Home Programs

Parent involvement in a family child care home or smaller program will differ in some ways from large center programs, but the most important consideration will be the same in both kinds of programs: Activities should meet the needs of the parents and caregivers involved. Here are some appropriate ways to encourage parent participation in either a center or a family child care home:

- Create a newsletter.
- Help parents of different families get together to meet basic domestic needs.
- Arrange social events that include the whole family.
- Encourage informal discussions when parents are in the child care setting.
- Let parents know their help is needed.

Create a Newsletter

A monthly newsletter can keep families and staff in touch and help foster a sense of community. If a parent in your program enjoys writing, ask him or her to help with the newsletter. Make it a cooperative venture. Items can be contributed by anyone in the program.

A newsletter can simply be a page or two of typed items, photocopied onto either white or colored paper. A catchy name and childlike drawing at the top increase the newsletter's appeal. Almost anything of interest to parents and caregivers of infants and toddlers can find its way into a newsletter. Humor, when used with sensitivity, can enhance the newsletter.

A well-written newsletter can keep families and staff informed about what is going on in the program and with one another. Use the newsletter to welcome new staff and families and say farewell to those who leave. Information about current health issues, changes in policy, notices about social events, or reminders about timely payment of fees can be communicated. However, the newsletter should not be the only source of important notices. Policy matters should always be discussed directly with parents, as well, to make certain they are clearly informed about them.

Special features of a newsletter may include:

1. A "Spotlight on Staff" column based on an interview with a different staff person each month
2. A "Parents' Column" written by a different parent every month
3. Important family events, such as births, graduations, reunions, and so forth
4. Information on infant or toddler development
5. Recipes and ideas for activities with infants and toddlers at home
6. A column of cute sayings by children in the program who are just beginning to talk
7. A "Help!" feature asking for volunteers to fix toys, organize a fund-raiser, or do whatever is needed
8. Notices of community events of special interest to parents and staff

Working Together on Basic Needs

Just making ends meet is a priority with many parents of infants and toddlers. The child care program can be a powerful force in helping parents meet basic needs, such as exchanging baby-sitting, looking for housing, and buying in bulk quantities. For some parents, working with other families may be the most effective way to help them feel involved. If caregivers work cooperatively with parents to solve their problems, the resulting partnerships will thrive.

Arranging Fun Family Events

Many parents, especially teenage parents, miss the fun they had before the baby was born. Because they cannot afford babysitters, they feel tied down. Activities that include the whole family, such as a picnic, video night, or party, may attract parents who would not be able to get away for a parent education meeting or an adults-only social event.

Encouraging Informal Discussions

Some of the most valuable suggestions and exchanges of information occur during informal conversations. Listen carefully to hear what the parent is really saying. For example, a mother remarked to a toddler caregiver, "I think some caregivers like to keep children in diapers because they don't want to bother with potty training. I don't want my child to still be in diapers at the end of this year when he will be three."

This parent wanted her child toilet trained and seemed uncertain that her concerns would be taken seriously. The caregiver listened carefully and heard her message loud and clear. She then followed up on the parent's comment. By sharing ideas, she and the parent came up with a plan for an appropriate and cooperative toilet learning effort.

You may feel that you would like to help a certain mother learn to talk with her baby more when she changes his diaper. You can demonstrate this informally while she is in the room. First, you can talk to the infant about his arms, his legs, and his kicking. Then glancing at the mother, you might say, "Isn't it wonderful how he responds to being talked to?" An interaction such as this is personal, relaxed, and acceptable to the parent. It is a much more effective way to handle the matter than a formal meeting in which you tell a group of parents, "Babies respond when you talk to them."

Letting Parents Know the Need for Help

Let parents and other family members know the many ways they are needed. Holding a crying baby, getting a snack ready, or helping out with recordkeeping are just a few of the ways an extra pair of hands can come to the rescue. In addition, many parents have special skills that they can contribute to your program, such as art, music, design, cooking, gardening, or carpentry.

Although most working parents will be unable to help out regularly with the children during the day, some may be able to visit the program from time to time. Let parents know that they are welcome in the program. Seeing their parents in child care talking, laughing, and working together with their caregivers is important for children. Participating once in a while in the day's activities, even if it is only for an hour or so, also helps parents who feel guilty or anxious about using child care become more comfortable with the situation.

Parent Involvement in Center Programs

Some approaches to involving parents in child care are more appropriate to bigger programs. The center's programs generally have larger staffs, more space, and a greater number of families for whom to plan group activities. Some types of participation more appropriate to a center's care include the following:

- Visiting families at home
- Making the center available during off hours
- Asking parents to help with repairs, improvements, and beautification of the child care environment
- Inviting parents to work in the program
- Having parents serve on an advisory or planning council

Visiting Families at Home

A quality infant/toddler center care program will try to build in time for home visits. Most parents welcome home visits, but new families usually need some time at first to become certain of the staff's respect and acceptance. Then they are likely to feel pleased that you are willing to visit them. Your personal interest in them will be appreciated.

Making home visits is an excellent way to learn more about the families in your program and thus strengthen your partnership. You will see the toys the infant or toddler plays with and the kind of space and opportunities for exploration or limits on exploration that the child has at home. Seeing the interaction of family members, their habits, and attitudes will also give you valuable insights. Your understanding of the child's behavior and needs will be enhanced and your suggestions to the parents will be more appropriate.

Informal visits at home with families can also lead to cordial relationships between you and family members. Here is how one caregiver expressed what a home visit meant to her:

> On the first home visit, I was understandably unsure of how far I could pursue my relationship with the Mills family. I decided to be as open as possible. I found that by allowing the family to set the tone of the relationship, instead of pushing my attitudes on them, I was able to gain much from the visit. I sense that we both had a really good feeling about it. I learned a lot just by listening, and Roma seemed to realize that I was genuinely interested. I want very much to continue making these types of visits and strengthening our bonds of friendship.

Making the Center Available During Off Hours

In addition to family social events, the child care facility can be made available one or two evenings a week for activities of interest to parents. One parent might be responsible for opening and closing the building; another, for leaving it ready to use the next morning.

For example, learning English is a high priority for many immigrant families. In the evenings the facility could be used for classes in English as a second language. Exercise classes, sewing, cooking, or craft workshops are activities that might interest some parents. The child care setting might also provide space during off hours for tutoring of older children by community volunteers. The possibilities are limited only by the needs and interests of families in the program.

Asking for Help with Maintenance

All of the work needed to keep a home in good repair is also needed in child care settings. Even more maintenance is needed because of heavy use by so many children and adults. Some parents whose schedules or preferences keep them from working in the program may be pleased to use their skills to help maintain the facility. Here are some ways parents can help:

1. Improve the outside area by planting new flowers and shrubs, reseeding grass, creating climbing mounds, and building new play structures for infants and toddlers.
2. Repair large play equipment.
3. Reorganize, clean, and straighten closets and shelves.
4. Help with laundry.
5. Sanitize toys and furniture.

If it is difficult for parents to get out, they may wish to do something at home, such as:

1. Make new toys from recycled materials.
2. Repair books or toys.
3. Make doll clothes.
4. Alter dressup clothes for dramatic play.
5. Cut out pictures from magazines for a collage and display.

Working in the Program

A large program will generally have a few parents who are available and interested in assisting with the children in the program. Caregivers need to help these parents have successful experiences from the beginning. The following are some of the ways parents can be eased into classrooms as helpers:

1. Set aside time to give parents a general overview of what is to be done in the program and when it should be done. Find out what the parents would feel comfortable doing at first. Be sure the parents are assigned this task.
2. Post a list each week showing which parent is responsible for what role. Begin by assigning simple tasks and express appreciation for what is done. Be ready to help, if necessary.

3. Avoid assigning only tedious tasks, especially at first. Let parents do something enjoyable. Later they will see that tasks, such as doing laundry, making copies and collating them, and cleaning up, are needed, and they will voluntarily take on those chores.
4. Keep the tasks varied so that the parent can "grow on the job." A parent may bottle-feed an infant for a few days, then get down on the floor with him or her to play. Soon the parent may feel comfortable reading the infant a book.
5. Help parents to recognize special abilities they may have in working with young children. Some parents may begin to see child care as a career opportunity. You can help the interested parent move toward becoming a professional by suggesting workshops, community college classes, and so on.

Forming a Parent Council

If parents are to be full-fledged partners, they should have a voice in making policy decisions. Many federal and state programs require parent councils. Some parents feel that they are not adequate to fill this role. At first you may have to settle for the participation of one or two parents on a committee with the program manager and staff representatives.

Helping parents develop their leadership skills and confidence is a challenging and rewarding task. From the beginning, all parents in the program should understand that the goal is to have a fully functioning council with many participants. The first committee members should avoid giving the impression that they have a privileged position. One of their roles, with support from program staff, will be to generate interest in the council and encourage more parents to become involved.

The development of a parent council might be the goal for the first year of a program's operation. During that year many decisions will be made, such as:

1. Identifying the role of the council
2. Setting up procedures for selection of members, determining length of terms and number of participants, arranging the staggering of terms, and ensuring representation of all groups
3. Establishing meeting times, frequency, place, and quorum needed
4. Dealing with issues suggested by parents

While the council is taking shape, those parents who are interested can be offered training in how to participate in a council, including how to conduct business in meetings.

Teenage Parent Involvement

Teenage parents have special needs. They are not yet physically or emotionally mature, and yet they have the responsibilities of an adult. The majority of teenage mothers are single parents with little or no contact with the baby's father. Usually, they live at home. Often, their own mothers were teenage parents. Many of them have low incomes and often have inadequate health care and nutrition during their pregnancies. They are a high-risk group.

Finishing high school is an important step for teenage parents. In order to do this, they need care for their infants and toddlers. The child care program should encourage teenage parents to complete high school. Some high schools provide infant/toddler care on the campus so that parents can come and visit their children during their breaks from class. Whether teenage parents participate in an infant/toddler care program specifically designed for them or one in which they are included with older parents, their needs require special consideration.

Teenage parents are often angered by being treated as immature. They may deeply resent the expression "babies having babies." The experience of giving birth often changes the way teenage mothers see themselves. Sometimes a teenage mother will seek emancipated

Respect the confidentiality of teenage parents.

status, a judgment by the courts that she is able to care for her baby on her own. She may ask for help from her caregiver when the courts hear the case. This can be a difficult situation for the caregiver as well as for the family.

Since most teenagers live at home, a program working with them also needs to involve their families. As teenagers learn from the child care program how to care for their infants, these ways, especially concerning discipline and feeding, may differ from the grandmother's approach. Unless the program involves grandmothers, conflicts may arise.

One way to involve grandmothers is to organize a group that meets once a month with caregivers and/or a counselor. This group can provide a means of discussing issues causing problems in the teenagers' homes without identifying the specific home. Some meetings can be for grandmothers only, while others may involve both grandmothers and teenage mothers. Such opportunities for communication can help ease many potentially tense situations.

In one program, teenage mothers were asked to write a letter expressing what they would like to say to a young girl about to have a baby. The following letter expresses the way many teenagers feel:

> Now you are going to be a mother and it is time to put away childish things. You will be quite lonely and afraid, but all this will vanish when they show you your precious bundle.
>
> If you are going to keep your baby, remember your job will be filled with many lonely and fear-filled times. But all things can be accomplished with faith. Try to remember that you need a night out. This helps to keep nerves and tension at a minimum and makes a better relationship for your child and you. Try and do as many things as possible with your child.

Questions Parents May Have About Their Involvement in Child Care

1. What are the different ways I can participate?
2. Will the caregiver(s) accept me?
3. Will I be able to bring my other children? Sometimes? Always?
4. Am I really needed?
5. Will I be treated with respect?
6. Will the caregiver listen to me?
7. Will my willingness to help be taken advantage of?
8. Will my participation really help my child?
9. Will someone tell me exactly what I am to do?
10. Will I work directly with my own child?

Offers a concise, step-by-step, proven strategy for coming to mutually acceptable agreements in every kind of conflict, whether it involves parents and children, neighbors, bosses and employees, customers, corporations, tenants, or diplomats. Based on studies and conferences conducted by the Harvard Negotiation Project, a group that deals with all levels of conflict resolution, from domestic to business to international disputes.

Gonzalez-Mena, Janet, and Dianne W. Eyer. *Infants, Toddlers, and Caregivers*. Mountain View, Calif.: Mayfield Publishing Co., 2001.

This expanded edition includes sections on parent-caregiver relationships and nine-month separation in child care and multicultural situations.

Greenman, James. "Beyond Family Friendly: The Family Center," *Child Care Information Exchange,* Vol. 114 (March/April 1997), 66–69.

Advocates the creation of family care centers that focus on the family's economic and psychological security and the relationships that promote well-being as well as on the child's security, health, and development.

A Head Start Handbook of the Parent Involvement Vision and Strategies. Washington, D.C.: Head Start Bureau, U.S. Department of Health and Human Services, 1996.

Presents Head Start's detailed guide to setting up the family component of any early childhood program, including planning and preparation, parenting involvement strategies, and managing transitions.

Miller, Karen. "Caring for the Little Ones—Developing a Collaborative Relationship with Parents," *Child Care Information Exchange*, Vol. 135 (September/October 2000), 86–88.

Discusses the benefits of collaborative relationships with parents and provides suggestions for developing rapport and offering support.

Schorr, Lizbeth B., and Daniel Schorr. *Within Our Reach: Breaking the Cycle of Disadvantage and Despair*. New York: Doubleday and Co., 1989.

Reviews intervention programs created over the past 20 years for young children at risk. Maintains that the nation already has the answers for providing appropriate educational intervention and support and does not need to reinvent strategies or approaches. Describes various methods of working with difficult issues and dysfunctional families.

Schweikert, Gigi. "I Confess, I've Changed—Confessions of a Child Care Provider and a Parent," *Child Care Information Exchange,* Vol. 111 (September/October 1996), 90–92.

Explores challenges in the communication between child care providers and parents through the eyes of a child care educator who is also a parent.

Schweikert, Gigi. "Remember Me? I'm the Other Parent—Insights for Meeting the Needs of Both Parents," *Child Care Information Exchange,* Vol. 126 (March/April 1999), 14–17.

Presents tips for meeting the needs of parents who are unable to see their children's teachers regularly. Focuses on the importance of providing accurate information and relying on various methods of communication.

Section Seven:
Conducting Business with Families

The business aspects of program operation are often troublesome for providers of infant/toddler care, whether they are in family child care homes or in centers. Caregivers and program managers rarely see themselves as business people. Frequently, their training in business procedures has been minimal. In addition, many caregivers rank humanitarian values over material ones. No wonder, then, that the business aspect of infant/toddler care can sometimes seem difficult.

Financial and Legal Matters

Most infant/toddler programs are unable to employ specialists to deal with business matters. In a family child care home, the caregiver is often program manager, custodian, and chief cook and bottle washer, too. The additional tasks of recordkeeping and budget balancing may seem overwhelming, but they are essential. Learning to conduct business with families in a firm yet flexible and friendly way will greatly strengthen your program.

Planning for Financial Returns

Some aspects of the child care business do not involve families directly but must be worked out before the program begins. One is learning how much to charge families so that you will be able to cover your costs and make a reasonable financial return. Make sure to include the costs of insurance, taxes, and possible audits when planning for a balanced budget. A good way to begin planning a realistic budget is to study the financial arrangements of other programs similar to the one you envision.

Planning a program requires careful thought and accurate information. Find out what types of services parents are looking for. You might consider expanding services by offering after-school care for older children or weekend care. The research you do should give you a realistic framework for the business aspects of your idea.

Later, you will be prepared to let families know why you charge what you

style of operations. Try to develop a friendly but assertive style.

You need to be straightforward, honest, and specific. These are attributes that can be developed. Self-help support groups for caregivers and program directors and assertiveness training workshops can help you to develop them. Such help is available in many local areas and can be well worth the investment of time and funds.

As you develop the ability to be friendly and flexible but firm, the payoff will be parents who know you care and yet know that you mean business. A businesslike approach will help to keep matters clear between caregivers and parents and eliminate unnecessary tension for all.

Points to Consider

1. Are you flexible but fair in business dealings with parents? Do parents know what you expect of them? Are you consistent in implementing program policies?
2. Are you assertive when dealing with parents about business matters? Do you sit down and talk with parents about being late with fees or picking up their child before the situation has become a serious problem? When it is necessary, do you face the need to terminate a family's enrollment?
3. Do you have realistic expectations of financial returns on your child care business based on research you have done? Have you considered expansion of services to include school-age children or evening/weekend child care? Are your fees reasonable compared with other programs of the same type and quality?
4. Have you consulted with a legal authority when creating your contract or parent-caregiver agreement? Do you have someone you can call on for legal advice from time to time?
5. What are some ways you can improve your ability to be flexible but firm? How can your communication about business matters be more effective?

Suggested Resources

Books and Articles

Buchanan, Teresa, and Diane Burts. "Getting Parents Involved in the 1990s," *Day Care and Early Education* (Summer 1995), 18–22.

Addresses the stress and mixed emotions often experienced by child care providers over parent involvement and some key elements for creating a context for family involvement.

Fisher, Roger, and William Ury. *Getting to Yes: Negotiating Agreement Without Giving In*. New York: Penguin Books, 1991.

Offers a concise, step-by-step, proven strategy for coming to mutually acceptable agreements in every kind of conflict, whether it involves parents and children, neighbors, bosses and employees, customers, corporations, tenants, or diplomats. Based on studies and conferences conducted by the Harvard Negotiation Project, a group that deals with all levels of conflict resolution, from domestic to business to international disputes.

Greenman, James. "Living in the Real World—Parent Partnerships: What They Don't Teach You Can Hurt," *Child Care Information Exchange*, Vol. 124 (November/December 1998), 78–82.

Discusses examples of difficulties for child care providers in developing parent partnerships and presents suggestions for creating successful relationships.

Modigliani, Kathy. *Parents Speak About Child Care* (Second edition). Boston, Mass.: Wheelock College Family Child Care Project, 1997.

Examines parent and family attitudes through 23 focus group discussions of parents' child care experiences in nine U.S. cities. Analyzes videotapes resulting from the project.

Stanley, Diane. "How to Defuse an Angry Parent," *Child Care Information Exchange,* Vol. 108 (March/April 1996), 34–35.

Offers a four-step plan for defusing a parent's anger: listen carefully; make sure the problem is well understood; acknowledge the parent's feelings; and explain the plan of action.

Section Eight:
Helping Families Under Stress

Family life can be stressful in today's busy world. If caring for infants and toddlers is to be a partnership with parents, professional caregivers must address the issue of family stress. At the same time, they cannot take on all the family problems with which parents are wrestling. What caregivers can do is show their concern by affirming and supporting the efforts of parents to be good parents.

In general, friendly attention can go a long way toward making an overloaded parent feel less alone. Here are some ways caregivers can help parents feel good about themselves:

1. Show an empathetic interest in the family and the family's situation.
2. Acknowledge the strengths and successes of the family.
3. Express appreciation to parents for thoughtful or helpful things they do.

Common Causes of Family Stress

You must decide whether the problems causing the stress are ones with which you are equipped to help or whether they require referral to other agencies. Learning about common causes of stress is the first step in making this decision.

"Hurry Sickness"

One common difficulty among parents who use infant/toddler care is "hurry sickness," which is caused by the lack of time to support both a career and a family life. Underlying the "hurry sickness" may be feelings of guilt and anxiety about not being perfect at either the workplace or home. A parent with "hurry sickness" often feels (1) overwhelmed by responsibilities; (2) physical tension; and (3) emotional tightness.

Since the amount of time cannot be increased, one way caregivers can help is by suggesting ways of managing time. For example, many parents put themselves and their children in a frenzy to leave on time in the mornings. In a friendly way, you can suggest to such parents that waking the whole family up a few minutes earlier might make getting ready easier. A parents' workshop on tips for hurried parents might be just the right way to make the following suggestions:

1. Lay out the children's clothes the night before. Let older children help younger children in picking out what they want to wear.
2. Get the diaper bag ready with a change of clothes the night before.
3. Prepare the coffee the night before so the coffee maker is ready to turn on in the morning.
4. Ask older children to help prepare breakfast and make lunches.

These small changes can make a big difference. Having help from the whole family creates a positive, cooperative atmosphere and starts the day with a good feeling for parents instead of one of breathless exhaustion.

Just as getting ready in the morning can go more smoothly, the hours after work can be organized so that one person, usually the mother, does not have to do everything. Parents will begin to come up with their own suggestions once they get the idea. Encouraging them to share their ideas will help other parents to manage their time better and, at the same time, increase the feeling of connection between families.

Tight Budgets

The majority of families using infant/toddler care must make sacrifices to afford quality care, and those families who qualify for state or federal assistance with child care fees generally have limited incomes.

Caregivers, many of them parents themselves, often have the same difficulties as the parents they serve in trying to stretch an inadequate salary to meet living expenses. Both parents and caregivers have much to gain from management sessions that teach them how to get more value for their money. Suggested topics are:

1. Making nutritious meals that cost less
2. Purchasing clothing and household equipment at discount stores
3. Exploring economical ways to shop for food
4. Using community sources for affordable housing
5. Learning to make simple repairs of household items

Once the subject of how to economize is introduced, parents will certainly come up with additional ideas. The infant/toddler program itself may want to become involved in activities, such as a clothing and toy exchange, cooperative buying, or a community garden.

Understanding Child Development

Child rearing is one area of stress for parents in which caregivers are uniquely qualified to help. The professional caregiver has an understanding of typical child development, experience caring for many young children, and personal knowledge of each child in the group. Those qualifications make caregivers an important resource for parents who have difficulty understanding or coping with their children's behavior or development.

For example, parents of infants often need reassurance that their baby is okay. Their mixed feelings about placing their infant in care often tend to amplify their fears about the baby's healthy development. You need not take these strong feelings personally when you understand the parents' underlying anxieties.

Using your rich experience with infants and toddlers, you can reassure parents when there is nothing to worry about. If something is amiss, you can help them with information and a referral to a specialist. You can also help anxious parents by sharing with them some humorous and interesting anecdotes about the babies.

A common source of stress for parents is having to adapt to changes in their child's behavior. Parents frequently are not prepared for the next stage in their child's growth. For example, when children leave infancy, they display a new array of behaviors. As infants become two-year-olds and gain a measure of independence, parents necessarily give up some control.

The new stage can be hard for parents to take, especially if they believe that their two-year-old is the only child behaving "that way." They may feel that something is wrong with the child, their parenting, or both. You can help parents learn more about the normal stages of development all children go through by providing information in a variety of ways.

Short, readable articles can be helpful to parents, but it is important to provide more than just reading materials. Videos are a popular source of information, with the advantage that parents can view them at their convenience in their homes. Some videos are recommended at the end of this section. Even more effective, if

Caregivers can encourage parents to help each other.

several parents seem interested, is for parents to form a discussion group about child behavior. Such a group can provide parents under stress with valuable mutual support.

In addition to offering parents child development information and support, infant/toddler caregivers, both in homes and in centers, should maintain a list of specialists to whom they can refer parents for consultation.

Here is an example of how a caregiver helped a parent who was worried about her child's development on her first visit to the program:

> Susan came into the Child Development Center carrying a nine-month-old infant. Kelly, the caregiver, could see that Susan was under severe stress. She greeted Susan cordially and learned that the baby's name was Carrie.
>
> KELLY: Maybe you would like to have Carrie sit on the floor and play with this toy?
>
> SUSAN: No, I'll just hold her. She's kind of clingy.
>
> Kelly guessed that Carrie was about nine months old. She explained to Susan that at nine months old many babies like to stay close to their mothers. Susan seemed reassured to

Four Steps to Resolving Issues with Parents

The video *Protective Urges: Working with the Feelings of Parents and Caregivers* recommends a four-step process for working with parents when problems arise:

1. **Explore your own feelings:** Be honest with yourself about how you feel about the situation. Recognize and accept your feelings. Focus on your own emotions rather than on the behavior of others.

2. **Check out your feelings with others:** Consult with other caregivers, program managers, or resource people. See if others share your concerns. Your discomfort may be a result of a cultural or personal difference rather than a question of right or wrong.

3. **Seek information from the parent:** To be sure that you are not misjudging the situation, find out why the parent is behaving in a particular way. Gather information but do not try to resolve the problem. Avoid criticizing, arguing, or disagreeing.

4. **Develop an action plan**

    A. Addressing your own issues

    - Get support—Seek specialized training, counseling, or just someone to talk with.
    - Handle your stress—Set aside time for yourself. Take walks, stretch, or meditate.
    - Set boundaries—When you feel you are doing too much to meet a family's needs, set specific limits.

    Sometimes, taking care of yourself will resolve the problem. At other times, you will need to go further and meet with parents.

    B. Interacting with parents

    - Reflect on the relationship—Is there tension between the two of you? Think about the parent's sensitivities and personality.
    - Decide on the content—Decide which are bottom-line issues and which ones are negotiable. Make notes of key points to bring up.
    - Plan the interaction—Select a quiet place and time. Think about how to present the topic so that the parent will not feel defensive. Stay open to the parent's point of view.

    Caregivers cannot solve everything on their own. Some problems are too big and require outside help.

    C. Finding outside help

    - Contact a resource and referral agency to see if support is available.
    - Refer parents to community services such as family support, drug and alcohol counseling, food bank, or health clinic.
    - Seek assistance through a child care mental health professional.

learn that her baby's clinginess was normal.

Although Kelly believed something more was worrying Susan, she waited until Susan felt ready to talk about it. Susan was finally able to express her deeper anxiety: She believed that Carrie's development was slow. She was not yet turning over, crawling, or showing an interest in toys.

Kelly suggested steps they could take together to learn more about what Carrie might need. The staff would observe her in the child care program, and Kelly would contact Carrie's doctor for more information. Finally, she recommended that Susan ask her doctor for a referral to a specialist for Carrie. Susan began to believe that there might be help for Carrie. She relaxed a little, lost some of her anxious look, and left with a new spring in her step.

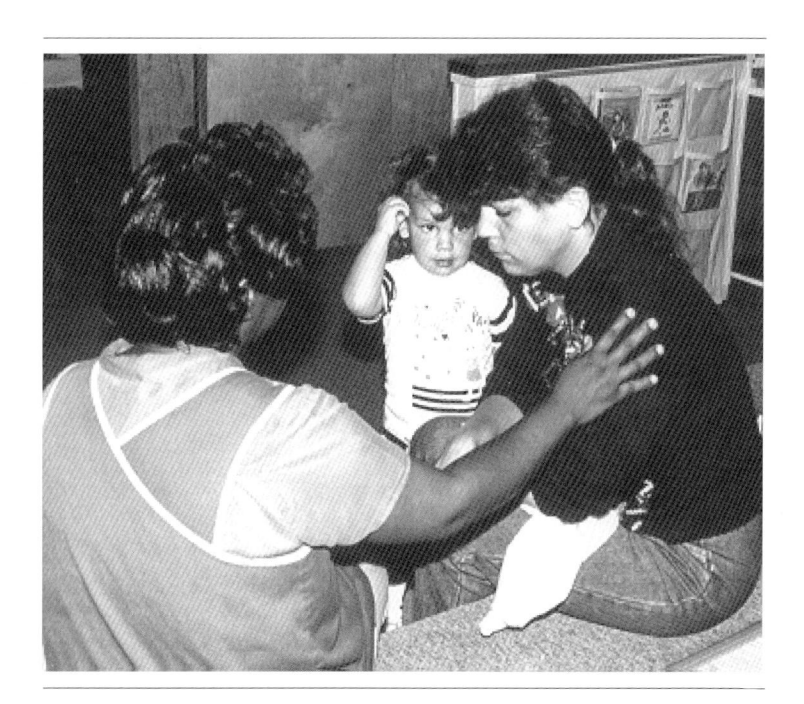

Worries About Health and Safety

Much of the anxiety of parents using infant/toddler care has to do with concern for their child's health and safety: "Is my baby getting enough attention or is he left lying all alone in his crib?" "Will Sonya's caregivers remember her milk allergy?" "Will Joan be sure to give Raymond the medication for his ear infection?"

The safety of the child, especially the increasingly active toddler, is often a matter of concern. Then, too, there is the nagging fear of sexual abuse. These anxieties cause real stress to parents and need to be discussed openly and honestly.

Again, it is important to avoid being defensive about parents' fears. No one is perfect, and caregivers have many things to keep in mind. He or she might forget a child's allergy to milk. Accidents do happen, even in the safest environment, although they should be few and minor if caregivers are attentive.

The best way to allay parents' anxieties is with information. Let parents know what your health and safety procedures are. Show them the place where you keep a list of children's allergies and medications. Be clear about your philosophy so that they will know you are aware of the needs of infants and toddlers, including their need for emotional support and attention.

Make sure parents have a chance to look around your environment and, when they do, point out the health and safety precautions that have been taken. Invite unscheduled visits and discuss the signs of child abuse. Above all, listen carefully to parents' expressions of concern and respond thoughtfully and sympathetically. Remember how you would feel (or have felt) entrusting your baby or toddler to someone you did not know well.

Family Crises

Family life can be demanding, especially for parents balancing the dual responsibilities of working outside the home and raising young children. Occasionally, a crisis can arise that threatens the family itself. Such crises may include a serious illness, the death of a close family member, or the loss of a job. Many families are able to stay together and carry on family functions until a crisis occurs. Then the crisis acts as an emotional valve that opens to release suppressed feelings. When the caregiver senses that a family is undergoing a crisis, the best thing to do is to refer parents to someone trained in crisis counseling.

Today in the United States, many marriages end in divorce, and a substantial number of divorces occur in families with very young children. Parents experiencing a divorce may turn to their child's caregiver to express feelings and find understanding.

Most parents will appreciate the support of their children's caregivers during especially stressful times. Caregivers can expand parents' opportunities for finding help by:

1. Being understanding and friendly
2. Putting parents with similar concerns in touch with one another, after checking with each parent to make sure that doing so would not violate the parents' need for confidentiality.
3. Encouraging a group of parents with similar problems to meet informally or with a professional trained in leading such groups, if they wish

Assisting parents in getting together with people who can help them is one of the most important things you can do. Sometimes parents just need someone to talk to. Listening to parents talk out their feelings is a great way to help reduce their stress.

Agencies Helping Families

Telephone directories usually include lists of services for families and children under "Social Service Organizations" and "Welfare Agencies." Most telephone books have the following information:

1. For emergency services, see the inside front cover of the directory or dial "0" or 911 if this emergency service is available in your area.

2. For child care services, look under:

    Child Care Services
    Nursery Schools
    Social Service Organizations
    Welfare Agencies

3. For child guidance or family relations counselors, look under:

    Marriage, Family and Child
        Counselors
    Mental Health Services
    Physicians (Psychiatrists)
    Psychologist Referral Service
    Psychologists
    Social Service Organizations
    Social Workers
    Welfare Agencies

4. For childbirth preparation or pregnancy counseling, look under:

    Educational Consultants
    Family Planning Information
    Maternal Child Health Services
    Social Service Organizations
    Women, Infant, and Child Nutrition
        Program

5. For divorce assistance, look under:

    Attorney Referral Service
    Attorneys
    Personal Services
    Social Service Organizations

6. For legal aid, look under:
   Attorney Referral Service
   Legal Aid Society
   Social Service Organizations
7. For economic guidance/family budget consultant, look under:
   Social Service Organizations
   Welfare Agencies
8. Telephone hot lines sometimes available are:
   Alcoholism Line
   Battered Women
   Child Abuse Life Line
   Child Health Information and Referral
   Children's Emergency Protective Services
   Drug Line
   Lawyer Referral Service
   Legal Aid Society
   Legal Assistance for Children
   Mental Health Information and Referral
   Parents Under Stress
   Public Works Action Line
   Sexual Trauma Center
   Suicide Prevention
   Telephone Aid in Living with Kids
   Women's Switchboard
   Youth Crisis Line

Points to Consider

1. Why is the support of parents undergoing stress such an important aspect of your partnership? How can you assist parents in developing the self-esteem necessary to deal with stress? How can you become a better listener, knowing that many parents have no one to talk to?
2. What are some ways you can involve family members to ease the pressure they feel? How can you build on the strengths of the families in your program? What are some ways you can encourage parents to help each other?
3. How can you assist parents under stress to find more effective ways of managing time and money?
4. Do you offer information and discussions on child development to parents? Are you generous with your reassurance of parents who feel anxious about your child care program? Do you suggest to parents that they sit down and talk with you whenever there may be unresolved tension or a problem?
5. Is the environment an open, friendly one designed for relaxation? Can you make it more relaxing by attending to the colors used, the decor, the kind of furniture, and the lighting?

Suggested Resources

Books and Articles

Behrstock, Barry B., and Richard Trubo. *The Parent's When-Not-to-Worry Book: Straight Talk About All Those Myths You've Learned from Your Parents, Friends—and Even Doctors.* New York: Harper & Row, 1981.

Provides help for parents who are concerned about using child care for their infants and toddlers.

Brazelton, T. Berry. *Working and Caring.* Boston, Mass.: Addison-Wesley Longman, 2000.

Provides helpful information for working parents and caregivers on the stresses working parents experience.

Brazelton, T. Berry, and Stanley I. Greenspan. *The Irreducible Needs of Children: What Every Child Must Have to Grow, Learn, and Flourish.* Boulder, Colo.: Perseus Book Group, 2000.

Explores seven needs of infants and young children that, when met by families and professional caregivers, provide the fundamental building blocks for children's higher-level emotional, social, and intellectual abilities.

Copeland, Margaret Leitch, and Barbara S. McCreedy. "Creating Family-Friendly Policies: Are Child Care Center Policies in Line with Current Family Realities?" *Child Care Information Exchange,* Vol. 113 (January/February 1997), 7–10.

Addresses current issues, such as corporate downsizing, flex time, and blended families, and the effects on emerging child care needs. Suggests that child care programs update policies by examining staff attitudes, evaluating enrollment policies, and offering more flexibility and support to parents.

Greenman, James. "Living in the Real World—Parent Partnerships: What They Don't Teach You Can Hurt," *Child Care Information Exchange*, Vol. 124 (November/December 1998), 78–82.

Discusses examples of difficulties for child care providers in developing parent partnerships and presents suggestions for creating successful relationships.

Honig, Alice Sterling. "Research in Review: Stress and Coping in Children" (Part 1), *Young Children,* Vol. 41, No. 4 (May 1986), 50–63.

Part 1 reviews research on the components and stages of stress in the lives of children, identifying six categories of stress factors: personal child variables, ecological stressors, socioeconomic status, catastrophes and terrors, family events, and spouse problems.

Honig, Alice Sterling. "Stress and Coping in Children: Interpersonal Family Relationships" (Part 2), *Young Children*, Vol. 41, No. 5 (July 1986), 47–59.

Part 2 reviews the interpersonal stresses between parents and children and describes ways for caregivers to enhance children's coping skills. A list of telltale signs of stress to alert parents and teachers is included.

Leavitt, Robin L., and Brenda K. Eheart. *Toddler Day Care: A Guide to Responsive Caregiving*. Lexington, Mass.: Lexington Books, 1985.

Comprehensive guide to various developmental aspects of toddler caregiving. Excellent chapter on separation and working with parents.

Powell, D. R. *Families and Early Childhood Programs*. Washington, D.C.: National Association for the Education of Young Children, 1989.

Describes how early childhood programs should respond to a dramatic new era of changing family structures and lifestyles. This stimulating monograph offers an in-depth, critical review of the growing literature on rationales for working with parents, on relations between families, on early childhood programs, and on promising strategies for addressing home-school relations. Available from the National Association for the Education of Young Children, 1509 16th Street NW, Washington, DC 20036.

Stanley, Diane. "How to Defuse an Angry Parent," *Child Care Information Exchange,* Vol. 108 (March/April 1996), 34–35.

Offers a four-step plan for defusing a parent's anger: listen carefully; make sure the problem is well understood;

acknowledge the parent's feelings; and explain the plan of action.

Warren, R. M. *Caring: Supporting Children's Growth.* Washington, D.C.: National Association for the Education of Young Children, 1977.

Suggests ways to help children deal with the challenges of growing up, including divorce, abuse, and death. Available from the National Association for the Education of Young Children, 1509 16th Street NW, Washington, DC 20036.

Section Nine:
Handling Difficult Issues

Difficult issues can arise in any infant/toddler care program. The most serious issues generally do not occur on a daily or weekly basis, but when they do occur, they must be dealt with promptly. In order to handle them successfully, a caregiver needs extra sensitivity, clarity of thought, communication skills, and goodwill.

Communicating About Difficult Issues

Discussing difficult issues in a constructive way is a necessary skill for caregivers. Difficulties usually concern the child's health, development, or behavior, or possibly a combination of all three. If you have shared good feelings and positive information on a day-to-day basis, these issues will not be so difficult to discuss. Such information will be heard in a context of mutual trust and concern for both parent and child.

Minor Injuries and Illness

One of the most difficult tasks for caregivers is to inform parents about an injury or illness of their child. Any accident that results in a child crying hard for a long time, a lump on the head, swelling, or profuse bleeding should be reported to the parent immediately. The parent should also be called whenever a child has symptoms of illness such as a fever, rash, diarrhea, excessive fussiness, and so on. Except in an emergency situation, the parent must make the decision of whether the child should be seen by a doctor.

In the case of an accident, caregivers should be prepared to explain in detail how it occurred. Express your genuine concern and regret that the child has been hurt, but remember that excessive apologies are not necessary. As long as the children were being properly supervised in a safe environment, most parents will understand that accidents can happen. Of course, if you find yourself making this type of phone call weekly or even monthly, it is a sign that your safety procedures may be inadequate and need improvement.

Working parents may be upset for several reasons when you call about an illness or injury. Their first concern will usually be for the child's welfare. In addition, however, they may be worried about their jobs. They could be in the middle of an important project at work or have run out of sick leave to cover such emergencies. The parent may have already been warned by employers about taking too much time from work to stay home with a sick child. The response to your news may be anger, impatience, or depression.

Do not take it personally when a parent has a negative response to bad news or assume that it means the parent does not care about the child. Working parents are under pressure to maintain a delicate balance between family needs and career needs. Your call may be like the proverbial straw that broke the camel's back.

The best approach is to begin with a statement of empathy for the parent's situation. You might say something like, "I'm sorry to have to call you at work. I know you must be busy, but I need to tell you that Rhea fell off the small slide and has quite a bump on her head. She seems okay, but I thought you might want to take her in to be checked by her pediatrician." Your statement shows concern for both the child and the parent and gives the parent the information needed to decide what to do.

Health or Development Issues

Caregivers become experts in recognizing the range of typical infant/toddler development. They see many babies go through stages of growth, each in his or her own way. From working with so many infants, caregivers often have an almost intuitive awareness when there may be a problem. For example, if a baby has not yet learned to turn over by nine months, the caregiver will try to discover why. One step is to talk about the problem with the parents. Any serious discussion of the child's development should include both parents, if appropriate. A time and place should be set up where you and the parents can sit comfortably without distractions.

Planning for such a meeting is important. Remember that an attitude of active listening supports parents and gives you the best opportunity to gather needed information. When raising questions about the child's progress, emphasize the benefits of early attention to potential developmental problems. The parents may already have been worried about the child's development and be feeling both frightened and relieved to begin dealing with it.

Caregivers are an important source of information for parents.

At that point, the parents will probably want to know what they should do. Your plan should include options for the parents for getting more information and assistance. Prepare in advance by gathering details about possible resources, including telephone numbers and addresses, costs, eligibility, and availability.

Families in such a situation often do not know about legally mandated special education services available to them. Suggest that they contact the local school district or discuss their concerns with their pediatrician and that they ask to be referred to a specialist. Express your readiness to help carry out the specialist's recommendations for treatment. Let the parents know that you understand how difficult the situation is for them. Caregivers can help parents find resources for the following problems with their child:

1. Vision
2. Hearing

3. Neurological development
4. Speech and cognitive development
5. Emotional disturbance
6. Physical disability
7. Chronic illness
8. Fetal alcohol syndrome
9. Drug exposure during mother's pregnancy

Once the problem has been identified and the family receives the appropriate services, a specialist may design a program to foster the child's development at home and in child care. Working together, parents and caregivers can provide the consistency needed for elimination or improvement of the problem. With this approach, bad news can be converted to good news for both parent and child.

Issues with Behavior

Normally, a program is able to handle behavior issues without bringing in the parent. Snatching toys, pushing, and hitting, for example, are typical behaviors of toddlers learning rudimentary social skills. Helping two-year-olds find acceptable ways of expressing feelings and desires is a basic part of toddler curriculum.

Occasionally, however, caregivers need to talk with parents about a child's behavior in the group. If a child's behavior is consistently inappropriate, the parent may be able to shed some light on it. When discussion of inappropriate child behavior is necessary, the following guidelines will help ensure a productive conversation:

1. Avoid greeting parents at the end of the day with a list of the child's negative behaviors.
2. Remember to handle tactfully information which the parent may perceive as negative about a child.
3. Find a quiet corner, sit down with the parent, and present the information as a problem to be solved together.

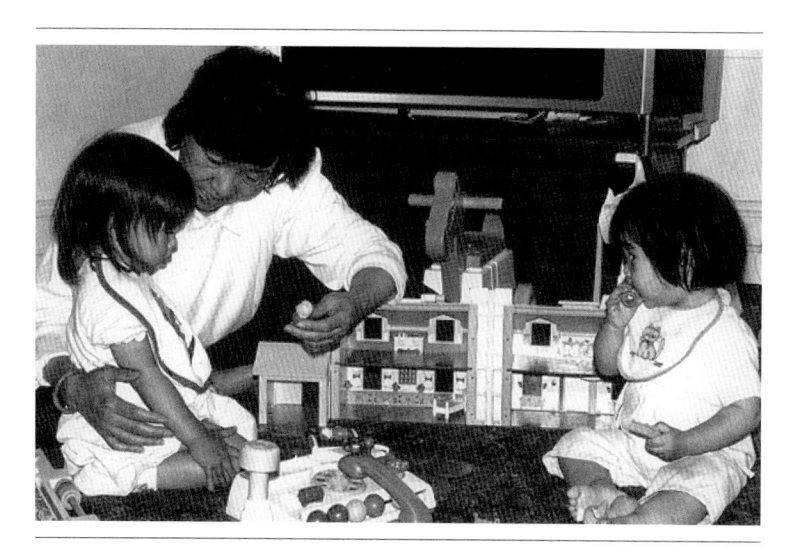

You might begin the discussion this way: "Eddie seems to have a hard time settling down to play with other children. Is there anything we can do to help him calm down? What's he like at home?" Suggest that a change in normal routines may help in correcting the problem. For instance, the parent can try spending more time alone with the toddler; the caregiver can try giving the child more individual attention when time permits.

Conversations should take place regularly with the parent of the child whose behavior is persistently inappropriate. Emphasize that biting and other aggressive behaviors are normal for children around two years old, but that the child needs help to learn more acceptable ways to express his or her needs. See whether you can identify a specific reason for the behavior. Sometimes a change in the child's life, such as a new infant in the family, will set off a phase of biting or other difficult behaviors.

When Other Parents Become Involved

Some behaviors, such as biting, may be so upsetting that other parents will become involved. Parents often become very angry when their child is bitten. They may be ready to have the aggressor "kicked out" immediately. If several parents are unhappy about a child's hurtful behavior, set up a meeting where the subject can be discussed. You can use the meeting to tell what you know about the problem in a calm and objective way:

1. Explain that toddlers sometimes go through a stage of biting or other aggressive behavior which they usually outgrow.

2. Describe your methods of protecting all children in the group by preventing the behavior before it occurs, such as staying close to the child who has a tendency to bite and inviting the child into well-supervised play activities.

3. Outline ways that you help children to redirect their actions which are potentially hurtful to others in the group.

4. Talk about your procedures after hurtful behavior occurs, such as comforting the child who was hurt and helping the aggressor to understand how much it hurts.

5 Express your awareness of toddlers' needs to:

   a. Have clear limits.
   b. Learn to solve their own problems with help from the caregiver.
   c. Have caregivers who are ready to help when needed.
   d. Develop a sense of self and sensitivity to others.

Finally, discuss with parents whether they would like to be faced with termination from the program if their child entered a phase of biting or other aggressive behavior. Usually, if parents feel they are being included in an effort to solve the problem, they will be more flexible and supportive of the program.

Problem behaviors, such as biting, are usually short-lived and can be resolved by a cooperative effort between parent and caregivers. Occasionally, a behavior is very disruptive to the group and, after exploring options with the parent, you may find that the situation does not improve. In this case, termination of the family from the program may be necessary. The two questions to ask yourself before coming to this difficult decision are:

1. Is it in the child's best interests to stay in the program?
2. Are other children being harmed?

Caregivers need to avoid being manipulated into allowing problems to go unattended. The problems become only more difficult as the child grows older.

Behavior problems that are serious enough to lead to termination in the program need to be attended to, not ignored.

Dealing with Mistreatment of Children

Some parents hurt their child with excessive yelling, with name-calling ("bad boy" or "bad girl"), with repeated threats that induce fear, by depriving the child of food as a punishment, or by exposing the child to adult behavior that is damaging for the child to witness. Problems like these have no easy prescription. The caregiver must be aware of the parent's temperament, life-style, and sensitivities in order to approach the subject tactfully. If a warm and mutually respectful relationship has already been developed, the interaction is more likely to succeed. The "we" approach, as shown in the following example, may be helpful to try:

A mother threatens her two-year-old son whenever he misbehaves. She often interprets his normal developmental growth as misbehavior. She tells him that if he hits his baby sister, "The monster is going to do something awful to you if you hit your sister again." She says the monster may take away his teddy bear, his favorite toy. The caregiver knows the threat is affecting the child. She waits for a time when she senses that the mother is more relaxed than usual. The mother did not have to go to work today, so she is visiting her son at child care. Mother and caregiver are sitting outside in the yard in a quiet place.

MOTHER: Oh, it is so good just to sit and not feel that I have to jump up to tend to something.

CAREGIVER: That is a great feeling, isn't it? I feel that way, too. Do you suppose that your son ever feels that way?

MOTHER: Oh, I doubt it. He's too young. Why did you think of such a thing?

CAREGIVER: Well, I notice that he seems kinda tied up in himself. He starts to do something and then he looks around as if he thinks maybe he shouldn't, as if someone were watching him. Is there something we could do that would help him to be more spontaneous, not so fearful?

MOTHER: I do have to correct him a lot. He seems bent on misbehaving. He's always hitting his baby sister. When I correct him, I'll find him in a corner tearing up a book. Then I have to scold him again.

CAREGIVER: Why do you think he likes to hit his sister? Is he trying to tell you something?

MOTHER: Hmm. Maybe he's jealous of his sister.

CAREGIVER: What could we do to help him? I wonder if you and I could come up with a plan together to help your son feel more free.

The mother and the caregiver worked out a plan in which she agreed to "no more threats, for a while, at least." Her son would have the opportunity to help with feeding his sister once a day for a few minutes. The mother would talk to him about what he does in child care and how much she loves him, spending a few minutes alone with him as she put him to bed. She would ignore minor infractions, at least for the time being. The caregiver agreed to work along the same lines, taking special time to observe and to play with him.

> *Be aware of signs of child abuse. Keep a written record of possible abuse.*

In two weeks they would talk again to see if there had been any improvement.

Another approach to helping parents learn better ways of dealing with their children is to recommend appropriate books or videos on infant and toddler development. You might also suggest attendance at a parenting workshop or parent support group. Larger programs sometimes develop their own series of parents' meetings where parents can share knowledge of their children with caregivers.

Inviting the parent who is mistreating his or her child to spend time in the program has great promise, if the parent can arrange it. This experience will give the parent firsthand knowledge that yelling, threatening, and scolding are not necessary to get positive behavior from infants and toddlers.

Child Abuse or Neglect

If you suspect that a child in your care is being abused by the parents or anyone else, you must take immediate action. Laws define abuse and neglect very specifically. The procedures for dealing with abuse or neglect are also specific.

The first step is detection. As a routine procedure when a parent brings a child to the child care setting, give the child a quick health inspection to be sure he or she is not ill. Children with infectious diseases should be sent home immediately. Any signs of neglect or of major abuse may be apparent at this time or they may become visible later when the child is undressed. Before suspecting the parents of child abuse, remember to consider the child's culture. Some cultures have medical practices, such as "coin rubbing," which is not necessarily harmful but can be mistaken for abuse because it may leave bruise-like marks.

The second step is documentation. If you see any sign of bruises, burn marks or dire neglect, make a mental note of it. Later, ask the parent about what you have noticed. Usually, there will be an explanation such as, "She fell down the stairs," or "She ran into my cigarette as I was holding it." These are, of course, possibilities. Make a written note of the condition of the child, the parent's explanation, and the date. The child should be observed carefully for any behavior that is different from usual.

If the signs of abuse are severe, report them right away. Most states require anyone who suspects child abuse to report it. You do not have to decide whether the child has been abused, only that you have enough reason to suspect abuse. Generally, the name of the reporter is not given, but in the case of a child care center it cannot be avoided.

If a questionable situation occurs again, you will need to inform the local child protection agency. Your role is to try to protect the child and to maintain confidentiality. No one in the program who is not directly involved should be told about the incident.

After the report, the child protection agency takes charge. An investigation will be made, and action may be taken to protect the child from the parent. When agencies outside the child care program enter the situation, procedures may occur that are uncomfortable for caregivers. For example, a law enforcement person may have to come to the program if the situation is serious.

You may also have to face the angry feelings of the reported parent. This is almost inevitable and is a necessary consequence of doing something which must be done. Your feelings of concern for the parent or fear of his or her reaction may tempt you to delay reporting what the evidence suggests. However, this is dangerous for the child and must be avoided.

Points to Consider

1. With sensitive issues, do you avoid making hasty decisions? Do you give yourself time to think through the consequences of any approach you are considering?
2. Are you careful to handle situations quietly, keeping information confidential? What steps can you take to deal with the problem of gossip among staff and/or families?
3. When there is a problem, do you tailor your handling of it to the personality of the parent while keeping fairness in mind? Are you able to take difficult actions such as terminating a family's enrollment or reporting child abuse, when necessary?
4. Do you remind yourself that no one is perfect and that people sometimes get in conflicts with each other? Are you able to offer an apology, when appropriate, or invite a sit-down chat to clear the air?
5. What are some ways you can learn to deal with situations that cannot be resolved? Do you keep your sense of humor? Do you remember the importance of making the experience in the program constructive and fun for everyone involved?

Suggested Resources

Books and Articles

Anderson, M. Parker. *Parent-Provider Partnerships: Families Matter.* Cambridge, Mass.: Harvard Family Research Project, 1998.

   Advances the concept of family-centered child care by addressing the development of the child and family together. Offers family support principles that build on family strengths and the community's culture and resources.

Balaban, Nancy. "The Role of the Child Care Professional in Caring for Infants, Toddlers, and Their Families," *Young Children*, Vol. 47 (July 1992), 66–71.

   Addresses major elements of the caregiver's role, such as comforting a child, sharing knowledge of appropriate expectations, and facilitating parent-child separations.

Fisher, Roger, and William Ury. *Getting to Yes: Negotiating Agreement Without Giving In.* New York: Penguin Books, 1991.

Offers a concise, step-by-step, proven strategy for coming to mutually acceptable agreements in every kind of conflict, whether it involves parents and children, neighbors, bosses and employees, customers, corporations, tenants, or diplomats. Based on studies and conferences conducted by the Harvard Negotiation Project, a group that deals with all levels of conflict resolution, from domestic to business to international disputes.

From Neurons to Neighborhoods: The Science of Early Childhood Development. Edited by Deborah A. Phillips and Jack Shonkoff. Washington, D.C.: National Academy Press, 2000.

Reports on an extensive review of scientific research and child policy centered on child development from birth to age five. Contains ten core concepts, including one that states: "Human development is shaped by a dynamic and continuous interaction between biology and experience."

Gordon, Joel. "Separation Anxiety: How to Ask a Family to Leave Your Center," *Child Care Information Exchange* (January 1988), 13–15.

Offers practical information on how to set a limit with a family for whom the program is not a good match and how to support staff in dealing with an uncomfortable situation.

Greenman, James. "Living in the Real World—Parent Partnerships: What They Don't Teach You Can Hurt," *Child Care Information Exchange*, Vol. 124 (November/December 1998), 78–82.

Discusses examples of difficulties for child care providers in developing parent partnerships and presents suggestions for creating successful relationships.

Infants: Their Social Environments. Edited by Bernice Weissbourd and Judith S. Musick. Washington, D.C.: National Association for the Education of Young Children, 1981.

Five chapters are especially important to caregivers in relating to parents: "A Parent Behavior Progression"; "The Mother's Project"; "Where Have All the Mothers Gone?"; "Supporting Parents as People"; and "Social Policy Affecting Infants."

Lerner, Claire, and Amy Laura Dombro. *Learning and Growing Together: Understanding and Supporting Your Child's Development*. Washington, D.C.: Zero to Three, 2000.

Offers four sections to support parents in their learning process: "How Parenthood Feels"; "Tuning In to Your Child"; "The Amazing First Three Years of Life"; "In Conclusion: Thoughts to Grow On."

O'Brien, Marion. *Inclusive Child Care for Infants and Toddlers: Meeting Individual and Special Needs*. Baltimore, Md.: Paul H. Brookes, 1997.

Provides a resource for infant/toddler caregivers in inclusive settings and a training guide for students and beginning teachers. Chapter 3 deals with parents as partners and suggests ways in which to communicate with family members and involve them in their children's care.

Powell, D. R. *Families and Early Childhood Programs*. Washington, D.C.: National Association for the Education of Young Children, 1989.

Describes how early childhood programs should respond to a dramatic new era of changing family structures and lifestyles. This stimulating monograph offers an in-depth, critical review of the growing literature on rationales for working with parents, on relations between families and early childhood programs, and on promising strategies for addressing home-school relations. Available from the National Association for the Education of Young Children, 1509 16th Street NW, Washington, DC 20036.

Schorr, Lizbeth B., and Daniel Schorr. *Within Our Reach: Breaking the Cycle of Disadvantage and Despair.* New York: Doubleday and Co., 1989.

Reviews intervention programs created over the past 20 years for young children at risk. Maintains that the nation already has the answers for providing appropriate educational intervention and support and does not need to reinvent strategies or approaches. Describes various methods of working with difficult issues and dysfunctional families.

Stanley, Diane. "How to Defuse an Angry Parent," *Child Care Information Exchange,* Vol. 108 (March/April 1996), 34–35.

Offers a four-step plan for defusing a parent's anger: listen carefully; make sure the problem is well understood; acknowledge the parent's feelings; and explain the plan of action.

MODULE I: Social–Emotional Growth and Socialization

Videos and Video Magazines:
- First Moves: Welcoming a Child to a New Caregiving Setting
- Flexible, Fearful, or Feisty: The Different Temperaments of Infants and Toddlers
- Getting in Tune: Creating Nurturing Relationships with Infants and Toddlers

Printed Materials:
- Infant/Toddler Caregiving: A Guide to Social–Emotional Growth and Socialization
- Module I Trainer's Manual

MODULE II: Group Care

Videos and Video Magazines:
- It's Not Just Routine: Feeding, Diapering, and Napping Infants and Toddlers (Second edition)
- Respectfully Yours: Magda Gerber's Approach to Professional Infant/Toddler Care
- Space to Grow: Creating a Child Care Environment for Infants and Toddlers (Second edition)
- Together in Care: Meeting the Intimacy Needs of Infants and Toddlers in Groups

Printed Materials:
- Infant/Toddler Caregiving: A Guide to Routines (Second edition)
- Infant/Toddler Caregiving: A Guide to Setting Up Environments
- Module II Trainer's Manual

MODULE III: Learning and Development

Videos and Video Magazines:
- The Ages of Infancy: Caring for Young, Mobile, and Older Infants
- Discoveries of Infancy: Cognitive Development and Learning
- Early Messages: Facilitating Language Development and Communication

Printed Materials:
- Infant/Toddler Caregiving: A Guide to Cognitive Development and Learning
- Infant/Toddler Caregiving: A Guide to Language Development and Communication
- Module III Trainer's Manual

MODULE IV: Culture, Family, and Providers

Videos and Video Magazines:
- Essential Connections: Ten Keys to Culturally Sensitive Child Care
- Protective Urges: Working with the Feelings of Parents and Caregivers

Printed Materials:
- Infant/Toddler Caregiving: A Guide to Creating Partnerships with Families
- Infant/Toddler Caregiving: A Guide to Culturally Sensitive Care
- Module IV Trainer's Manual

New prices effective December 2004

ORDER FORM

New prices effective December 2004

Module I: Social–Emotional Growth and Socialization

Title	Item no.	Quantity	Price	Total
First Moves - English video (1988)	0751		$75.00	
First Moves - Spanish video (1988)	0771		75.00	
First Moves - Chinese (Cantonese) video (1988)	0772		75.00	
First Moves - PAL English video (1988)	1416		75.00	
Flexible, Fearful, or Feisty - English video (1990)	0839		75.00	
Flexible, Fearful, or Feisty - Spanish video (1990)	0872		75.00	
Flexible, Fearful, or Feisty - Chinese (Cantonese) video (1990)	0871		75.00	
Flexible, Fearful, or Feisty - PAL English video (1990)	1417		75.00	
Getting in Tune - English video (1990)	0809		75.00	
Getting in Tune - Spanish video (1990)	0811		75.00	
Getting in Tune - Chinese (Cantonese) video (1990)	0810		75.00	
Getting in Tune - PAL English video (1990)	1418		75.00	
Infant/Toddler Caregiving: A Guide to Social–Emotional Growth and Socialization	0876		18.00	
Module I Trainer's Manual	1084		25.00	
Module I: Social–Emotional Growth and Socialization (The package price includes 3 videos, 3 accompanying video magazines, 1 curriculum guide, and 1 trainer's manual.)			**Special price**	
English videos	9928		**239.00**	
Spanish videos	9929		**239.00**	
Chinese (Cantonese) videos	9930		**239.00**	
PAL English videos	9728		**239.00**	

Module II: Group Care

Title	Item no.	Quantity	Price	Total
It's Not Just Routine - (Second edition) English video (2000)	1483		75.00	
It's Not Just Routine - (Second edition) Spanish video (2000)	1484		75.00	
It's Not Just Routine - (Second edition) Chinese (Cantonese) video (2000)	1485		75.00	
It's Not Just Routine - (Second edition) PAL English video (2000)	1506		75.00	
Respectfully Yours - English video (1988)	0753		75.00	
Respectfully Yours - Spanish video (1988)	0773		75.00	
Respectfully Yours - Chinese (Cantonese) video (1988)	0774		75.00	
Respectfully Yours - PAL English video (1988)	1422		75.00	
Space to Grow - (Second edition) English video (2004)	1595		75.00	
Space to Grow - (Second edition) Spanish video (2004)	1596		75.00	
Space to Grow - PAL English video (2004)	1423		75.00	
Together in Care - English video (1992)	1044		75.00	
Together in Care - Spanish video (1992)	0888		75.00	
Together in Care - Chinese (Cantonese) video (1992)	1051		75.00	
Together in Care - PAL English video (1992)	1424		75.00	
Infant/Toddler Caregiving: A Guide to Routines (Second edition)	1510		18.00	
Infant/Toddler Caregiving: A Guide to Setting Up Environments	0879		18.00	
Module II Trainer's Manual	1076		25.00	
Module II: Group Care (The package price includes 4 videos, 4 accompanying video magazines, 2 curriculum guides, and 1 trainer's manual.)			**Special price**	
English videos	9931		**319.00**	
Spanish videos	9932		**319.00**	
Chinese (Cantonese) videos (Does not include Space to Grow video)	9933		**249.00**	
PAL English videos	9729		**319.00**	

Note: All videos include a video magazine in English.

New prices effective December 2004

Title	Item no.	Quantity	Price	Total
The Ages of Infancy - English video (1990)	0883		$75.00	
The Ages of Infancy - Spanish video (1990)	0884		75.00	
The Ages of Infancy - Chinese (Cantonese) video (1990)	0885		75.00	
The Ages of Infancy - PAL English video (1990)	1413		75.00	
Discoveries of Infancy - English video (1992)	1045		75.00	
Discoveries of Infancy - Spanish video (1992)	0829		75.00	
Discoveries of Infancy - Chinese (Cantonese) video (1992)	0784		75.00	
Discoveries of Infancy - PAL English video (1992)	1414		75.00	
Early Messages - English video (1998)	1425		75.00	
Early Messages - Spanish video (1998)	1446		75.00	
Early Messages - Chinese (Cantonese) video (1998)	1447		75.00	
Early Messages - PAL English video (1998)	1426		75.00	
Infant/Toddler Caregiving: A Guide to Cognitive Development and Learning	1055		18.00	
Infant/Toddler Caregiving: A Guide to Language Development and Communication	0880		18.00	
Module III Trainer's Manual	1108		25.00	
Module III: Learning and Development (The package price includes 3 videos, 3 accompanying video magazines, 2 curriculum guides, and 1 trainer's manual.)			**Special price**	
English videos	9860		**249.00**	
Spanish videos	9861		**249.00**	
Chinese (Cantonese) videos	9862		**249.00**	
PAL English videos	9730		**249.00**	

Module III: Learning and Development

Title	Item no.	Quantity	Price	Total
Essential Connections - English video (1993)	1056		75.00	
Essential Connections - Spanish video (1993)	1058		75.00	
Essential Connections - Chinese (Cantonese) video (1993)	1059		75.00	
Essential Connections - PAL English video (1993)	1415		75.00	
Protective Urges - English video (1996)	1270		75.00	
Protective Urges - Spanish video (1996)	1271		75.00	
Protective Urges - Chinese (Cantonese) video (1996)	1272		75.00	
Protective Urges - PAL English video (1996)	1421		75.00	
Infant/Toddler Caregiving: A Guide to Creating Partnerships with Families	0878		18.00	
Infant/Toddler Caregiving: A Guide to Culturally Sensitive Care	1057		18.00	
Module IV Trainer's Manual	1109		25.00	
Module IV: Culture, Family, and Providers (The package price includes 2 videos, 2 accompanying video magazines, 2 curriculum guides, and 1 trainer's manual.)			**Special price**	
English videos	9774		**189.00**	
Spanish videos	9775		**189.00**	
Chinese (Cantonese) videos	9776		**189.00**	
PAL English videos	9731		**189.00**	

Module IV: Culture, Family, and Providers

Title	Item no.	Quantity	Price	Total
Talking Points for Essential Connections - English video (1998)	1370		35.00	
Talking Points for Essential Connections - PAL English video (1998)	1427		35.00	
Talking Points for Protective Urges - English video (1998)	1369		25.00	
Talking Points for Protective Urges - PAL English video (1998)	1428		25.00	
Talking Points for Essential Connections - 50 video magazines (English)	9744		23.00	
Talking Points for Protective Urges - 50 video magazines (English)	9743		23.00	
Addendum to Trainer's Manuals I, II, III, IV: Spanish handouts/transparencies	1395		25.00	
The Family Day Care Supplement to Trainer's Manuals	7096		25.00	
In Our Hands - English video (1997)	1432		25.00	
In Our Hands - PAL English video (1997)	1419		25.00	
In Our Hands - 50 video magazines (English) (1997)	9747		23.00	
The Next Step - English video, 22 minutes (2004)	1554		75.00	
The Next Step - Spanish video, 22 minutes (2004)	1593		75.00	
The Next Step - English video, 8.5 minutes (2004)	1594		25.00	
The Next Step - 50 video magazines (English)	9711		23.00	

Additional Materials Available in The Program

91

New prices effective December 2004

Video Magazines

Title	Item no.	Quantity	Price	Total
The Ages of Infancy - 50 video magazines (English)	9954		$23.00	
The Ages of Infancy - 50 video magazines (Spanish)	9732		23.00	
Discoveries of Infancy - 50 video magazines (English)	9874		23.00	
Discoveries of Infancy - 50 video magazines (Spanish)	9733		23.00	
Early Messages - 50 video magazines (English)	9747		23.00	
Early Messages - 50 video magazines (Spanish)	9734		23.00	
Essential Connections - 50 video magazines (English)	9869		23.00	
Essential Connections - 50 video magazines (Spanish)	9735		23.00	
First Moves - 50 video magazines (English)	9960		23.00	
First Moves - 50 video magazines (Spanish)	9736		23.00	
Flexible, Fearful, or Feisty - 50 video magazines (English)	9956		23.00	
Flexible, Fearful, or Feisty - 50 video magazines (Spanish)	9737		23.00	
Getting in Tune - 50 video magazines (English)	9957		23.00	
Getting in Tune - 50 video magazines (Spanish)	9738		23.00	
It's Not Just Routine - 50 video magazines (Second edition) (English)	9724		23.00	
It's Not Just Routine - 50 video magazines (Second edition) (Spanish)	9723		23.00	
Protective Urges - 50 video magazines (English)	9778		23.00	
Protective Urges - 50 video magazines (Spanish)	9739		23.00	
Respectfully Yours - 50 video magazines (English)	9958		23.00	
Respectfully Yours - 50 video magazines (Spanish)	9740		23.00	
Space to Grow - 50 video magazines (Second edition) (English)	9709		23.00	
Space to Grow - 50 video magazines (Second edition) (Spanish)	9710		23.00	
Together in Care - 50 video magazines (English)	9873		23.00	
Together in Care - 50 video magazines (Spanish)	9742		23.00	
Sampler pack of 3 video magazines for each video in Modules I, II, III, and IV (English)	9720		23.00	
Sampler pack of 3 video magazines for each video in Modules I, II, III, and IV (Spanish)	9719		23.00	

Order Form

To order call: 1-800-995-4099 BUSINESS HOURS: 8:00 A.M.–4:30 P.M., PST
MONDAY THROUGH FRIDAY • FAX 916-323-0823

SUBTOTAL $ _____
California residents add sales tax. _____
Shipping and handling charges (See chart.) _____
TOTAL $ _____

NAME/ATTENTION _____

ADDRESS _____

CITY _____ STATE _____ ZIP CODE _____

(___) _____

COUNTY _____ DAYTIME TELEPHONE _____

PAYMENT METHOD:
☐ CHECK (Payable to California Department of Education)
☐ VISA
☐ MASTERCARD
☐ PURCHASE ORDER

CREDIT CARD NUMBER _____

EXPIRATION DATE _____

AUTHORIZED SIGNATURE _____

No. of Items	Shipping and Handling Charges
1	$3.00
2 - 50	$2.00 per order plus $1.00 per item
51+	Call 1-800-995-4099 for discounted rate

All orders to be delivered within the continental United States are shipped via United Parcel Service (UPS), ground service, ONLY.

UPS requires a street address.

Note: Shipping and handling charges for modules are $5.95 for each module.

Orders to Hawaii and Alaska are shipped via UPS Second Day Air. An additional charge for the shipping cost to those states plus a handling fee will be added to your credit card order.

Visit our Web site: **http://www.cde.ca.gov**

☐ **Please send me a free copy of the current *Educational Resources Catalog*.**

Mail completed order form to:
**California Department of Education
CDE Press Sales Office
1430 N Street, Suite 3207
Sacramento, CA 95814-5901**

Or fax completed order form to: **916-323-0823**

Note: Mail orders must be accompanied by a check, a purchase order, or a VISA or MasterCard credit card number, including expiration date and your signature. Purchase orders without checks are accepted from educational institutions, businesses, and governmental agencies. Purchase orders and credit card orders may be placed by FAX (916) 323-0823. Telephone orders will be accepted toll-free (1-800-995-4099) for credit card purchases. Please do not send cash. Stated prices are subject to change. Please order carefully; include correct item number and quantity for each publication ordered. All sales are final after 30 days.